D0841243

I AM THE ANCESTOR

Dedicated to:

To my Creator, to my Father... to my God!

Forever I've known that you have spared me. My personal prayer is from a humbling season in my life, it has always SAVED ME.

This day I need it the most:

Lord, for I KNOW that my life will have
MANY trials and tribulations,
PLEASE LORD, CONTINUE GRANTING ME
THE ABILITY TO ABSORB,
UNDERSTAND YOUR WILL AND TO

PERSEVERE THROUGH IT ALL.

"My Family"

M.G.R.A.J. for Life

Know this, "I AM" your mother. I may not be a daughter, a sister, an aunt, a cousin or a niece. But, "I AM" your mother. I take my ONLY role very seriously, which you all have learned and said. You know that I love each of you as my "FAVORITE". I am beyond grateful that you guys are in my life. It may have appeared to be very difficult at times, but that's life for everyone. With every breath that I was gifted, it was a breath that I took for you. For as long as I 'm allowed to breathe, I will for you. I thank you for taking this journey with me and I ask you now to embark on our next path..................TOGETHER as THE MGRAJ TREE continues.

Love: Mom, Mother, Ma'am, Mommy...MO

CONTENTS

ACKNOWLEDGEMENTS

'M SURE YOU WOULD AGREE THAT THE JOURNEY OF REFLEC-tion and self-evaluation serves you well in business and in life. With that being said, many people have been influential in the development of this book with me.

Stylz 220 Founder and CEO Brandy Collins, you have been a big support with helping me get this huge part of my life off the ground. From involving yourself, your parents, your husband, and your 2 children in many different fundraisers, to doing my hair and make-up for every interview and speaking engagement. There is no way to express my gratitude

to you for the compassion that you showed me other than saying Thank you. I will forever hear the sound in my ear as you're covering the same bald spots for over 13 years for you to say, "Monique, I will not allow you to do this alone I will be there for you". Though you are classified as a small business in this industry know that you will forever be M=my Corporate Sponsor

Secondly, to my bestfriend Rosalyn McKinney who has been near and dear to my heart for over 20 years. You have truly held a strong role of SISTER in my life for all the panic attacks, sleepless nights, heart wrenching conversations, and we both should take stock in a huge tissue manufactorer. Thank you for4LIFE.

Last, but not least, thanks goes to you Robert L. Smith unbeknowence to you, you were a life saver in many ways I salute you and grant you a purple heart as you were awarded for serving our country, but this one is from me just because you were there.

INTRODUCTION

I AM KNOWN BY MY "FAMILY" AND FRIENDS AS SYMBOLIE Monique Smith—sometimes. I think I am 43, 44, or 45 years of age. I was abducted from my biological family around the tender age of two. The year was 1968 or 1969. As an abductee, I have no accurate records for myself. My birth certificates (plural) have several different names and my social security card does, too. Since these were used to register me for school and as a means to receive various services as a child, the applications reflect the same wrong information.

In 1990 or so, it dawned on me that Symbolie Monique Smith may not even be my real name. It was more than likely pieced together by the woman I've know to be my mother all of my life. For this reason, I consider myself to be the genesis, the beginning of my family. I'm sure you're wondering, "Well, how can that be? We all come from somewhere."

That is true. The question for me, however, is "From where did I come?" Before I delve into that, allow me to share just a little bit about myself, and my life.

I am the proud mother of four healthy and intelligent children. My two daughters are named Courtney and Katlyn and my two sons are named Christopher and Xavier. I can never find enough words to really describe my love for them. They are just as much alike as they are different and connect with me in their own unique way. Each of them has found a way to use their gifts and talents to better themselves and bless someone else along the way. They have really made me proud to be their mother.

The time I spend with them is always quality time and very satisfying. I enjoy the motherly talks and taking a nice stroll with them through the mall or at a park. I am always looking for ways we can learn together because it really helps to strengthen our bond. It does not matter how big or small the opportunity is because it is always time well spent. Although I love being with them, I work hard to make sure they have their space. I know how important it is for children to engage with their peers, too.

My oldest daughter, Courtney, is in her fourth year of college. She is 20 years old and always on her "A" game with honors while riding on a four year scholarship. Courtney is my right hand and always there to lend any type of support she can. Sometimes, she acts like she is the mother of our family, making sure that her siblings are fine. She comes home from school on most weekends just to be there for us. Courtney is a wonderful daughter and what I would really consider the perfect first child. She handles her role as the oldest very seriously. When she turned 18, I immediately turned all of my important documents over to her. Every bank account, life insurance policies, deeds to the homes, and anything that has to do with my estate was given to her for safe keeping in the event something happens to me.

Courtney is the type of child you read about who at the age nine thinks her mom is the best and as a teenager does not want to be bothered with her mom. But, by the time she is 30 years old only wants to talk to her mom when things are going wrong and by the time she is 70 years old she wishes her mom was still alive. Courtney has made it perfectly clear that if anything happened to me, she will take care of the children while still going to college. She promised me that she would not drop out of college because she understands how important it is to get an education.

My son, Christopher, is what I would consider the perfect son. He is a senior in high school, has an impressive twelve years of perfect attendance, and has never given me one ounce of trouble. That's quite grand for a 17 year old black male in the Baltimore Public School System. He, too, has a high grade average which is enough to make any mother proud at every PTA meeting.

Because he felt internal pressure to be like his sister, he was striving at one point to excel as much as she had. But, when he realized he had to walk in his own shoes, he really began to embrace who he is and worked hard to build himself up.

Christopher has been totally exposed to every possible opportunity imaginable. He has experienced horseback riding, dirt bikes, swimming, archery – you name it, Christopher has done it with excellence and has taken it to the next level. The minute he mentions something he wants to try, he is ready. He does not have one favorite activity Christopher is a gentleman who will open the door for a lady and takes his role as the man of the house very, very seriously. My son truly has a big heart and is the one that can generally pull us all together to do a household task like raking leaves. I really cherish him and I hope he knows that.

My 12 year old, middle school son, Xavier, is following in the educational footsteps of his siblings. Even though life threw us a very serious curve ball last year, we managed to make it to home plate and not miss a single step. Xavier is truly in a class all by himself. He thinks for himself and does not get tempted to follow the crowd...even if that crowd is his mother and siblings. Xavier has been known to let the rest of us hang out while he stays home. That's just Xavier and I allow him to be himself. He is the child we know as "the one man show". He's not the "let's do this together" type of child. Once we were all raking leaves and here he comes outside to help us...after we were finished.

I AM THE ANCESTOR

When he wants to really be alone, Xavier goes inside of the bathroom. There, he knows no one will disturb him. He has one friend and does not run with groups or in packs. He plays chess, the flute, knows where he wants to go in life, and is on a really great track. He loves mommy time. Every month I rotate with each child so they can have one on one time with me. He is a mommy's boy to a certain extent, but he is also very strong and independent. He's very funny and so introverted. Sometimes when we are out as a family, he will have a look on his face that says, "Am I really a part of this family?" The rest of us are very outgoing.

Lastly Katlyn, my baby girl, is in elementary school. She is all of ten years old but acts more like she is 20 years old. I probably shouldn't call her a baby for she is extremely mature. Katlyn is a force to be reckoned with and a bit of a tomboy as the younger sister of two older brothers! Tomboy or not, she will toggle back down to getting her nails and hair done and loves to be in the kitchen with me. If she is in the mood to hang out, she'll hang out. If she's not in the mood to hang out, she won't pretend that she is just to make you happy. I love that honest side of her.

Katlyn has never given me problems. She is extremely smart and loves to read and write. I truly witnessed her creative skills when she hosted her first community workshop. That was a fun event and the community really came to show their support of Katlyn. She has never missed a day of school either and keeps her name on the honor roll. These days, she is really my little shadow and I enjoy our time together.

All their lives, my children have only known me as Monique Smith. It is really a shocker to them to hear me called "Symbolie" by people that I have known since I was a child. They had never asked why I don't use my first name and up until now they did not know. When someone learns of my first name and is curious enough to ask why I don't use it, I tell them that it's much easier to use my middle name and very time consuming to correct those who mispronounce my first name. Besides, "Monique" works so much better for public relations purposes.

I have been working in managerial positions at leading organizations for the past 20 years. Often, I would be the youngest, non-degreed employee in my department but would find myself getting promoted amongst my peers who had attained their degrees. This work ethic must have been instilled within me as a child. I began working around the age of 12 or 13 and have worked ever since. When I became a young adult, I began working through a temp agency as a mailroom clerk for a very prestigious medical facility. From there, I was promoted to a trainee and then to Senior Medical Claim Processor, all within one year. For the next fifteen years, I continued to work hard and as a result, promoted to Senior Claims Manager.

I resigned from that job in 2004 and began working for a very small construction company shortly thereafter. When I started, it was just the owner, myself, and a few day laborers hired as needed to perform various tasks. Over time, this $150,000 company grew from "one man, one van" in 2004 to an empire worth over five million dollars in 2010. I will never forget the day I met with three different financial institutions that were fighting to give me a loan for $2.7 million for a commercial building with lots of equity! I've seen plenty of fights in my day, but I had never seen a corporate conference room fight. Not a single punch was thrown but two of those lending institutions were down for the count. It was obviously painful. When I closed that deal I knew that I had the knack for running a very successful business!

I am now the owner of multiple residential properties. I purchased my first investment home for pennies, literally, in 1993. Because I was determined to not hire a property manager, I went to the library and read up on everything that pertained to being a landlord. I learned what the law was regarding rentals, downloaded and printed a lease, bought a "FOR RENT" sign from a major home improvement store, and rented it to a pretty decent tenant. I really lucked out with the tenant considering all the horror stories I've heard about rental their property. Anyway, I charged enough rent to pay off the mortgage in 2010. Now, the rent I collect from that property adequately covers the mortgage on the house I reside in presently.

My credit is fantastic! I do not have a single credit card and no equity loans. I pay cash for everything and enjoy a debt free life! When other folk in my neighborhood was racking up those low interest, introductory financing cards and purchasing everything from cars to candy, I ran in the other direction. I saw what those credit card companies were trying to do and I was not about to get trapped like so many others.

My life as a single parent is pretty typical. There is lots of homework, cooking, cleaning, and after-school activities like the chess club for my son. I volunteer for the PTA and Girl Scouts and facilitate a girls group at my son's high school. My community outreach is in the form of connecting with other women who I am positively influencing and encouraging to move forward in their lives. Sometimes we all get stuck and just need a gentle nudge to help us get back on track. I can relate very well to what they are going through. I consider every child I see one who needs love and nurturing. My "it takes a village" mentality drives me to really pour into them sometimes to a fault. When it comes to children and making sure they have what they need, I struggle to keep a balance. I just don't like to see them lacking anything. Even though I do what I do from my heart, the community, in turn, gifts so much back to me through delicious cakes and other neighborly acts.

Throughout all of this, I still make time for myself. I have to! My social life is pretty average for a woman who has her children's best interest first. Over the years, I've dated and enjoyed hobbies like sewing and knitting. I also make time to connect with other women at social events and outings. On a monthly basis, I attend a recurring women's event and every time I leave I am pumped and charged to work even harder. By all accounts, I feel like the most powerful woman in the world when I take into consideration what I have vs. what statistics report I should have.

Unfortunately, I am also a woman without a true identity on a quest to find out where it all began for me. Imagine a world with no links, no attachments, and no existence. Can you picture yourself walking down the street wondering if the person who just passed you is your brother, sister, or cousin? Do you know what it's like to get tested more frequently than most persons because of an unknown family medical history? Have you experienced not being able to enjoy a simple cruise to Aruba, Jamaica, or the Mediterranean because you cannot produce proof of your identity? I can't obtain a passport because my vital statistics are not correct. For too many years, I have lived this way and still I have no real answers. This is the reason I gave birth to I Am the Ancestor. After 15 years of endlessly searching for the truth, I suddenly realized that I must tell my story before I die in an attempt to leave behind a true legacy for my four children. Leaving this burden on Courtney is completely unacceptable to me.

I Am the Ancestor is an inspirational account of my life as a woman living in a world without a single connection. Thanks to being abducted, exploited, and raised by a woman named Tammie Smith who never showed any love and various municipalities such as the public school system, the Department of Social Security, Bureau of Vital Records, the Federal Bureau of Investigation, and police departments who dropped the ball at one point or another in my life, I am like many victims of abduction: left to put the pieces of my life together. What's worse is the impact this is having on my children. Now, it's my duty as a mother, the only dear title that I really have—for I'm not a daughter, a sister, an aunt, nor a cousin—to make sense of my history.

With this book, I truly want to share my strengths, expose my weaknesses, develop in all areas of my life, and survive by any means for my children and myself. When this book is finally released, I will be free, my children will be empowered, and the minds of many will be wide open! Not only that, but this book will open the door for other people in the world, like me, who are determined to put together the missing pieces of their lives. I believe that there are thousands, if not millions, of people like me in the world! As a matter of fact, just recently I saw two different news accounts of women who had been abducted as children and were reunited with their family. It shocked the world to know that we, adults who were abducted as children, are still out here.

Let me be clear. I am not on a quest to reconnect with any of the key players you will read about, and by no means am I reaching out to anyone to reunite me with long lost family members. Please understand that my past missions of this kind do not equate with the many reasons I am writing this book. Through tons of disappointments, I have learned the hard way that good intentions can yield unfortunate outcomes often times. I have learned from those mistakes, and I am determined to do things differently moving forward.

The only reason I am writing <u>I Am the Ancestor</u> is because this book will be a way for me to share with my children the life's identity of their mother and make them aware of our unidentifiable past while touching the soul of every possible role player.

ONE

The Blessings; Soaring High on all of My Dreams: "Cause I'm a Mom"

CLEARLY REMEMBER THE DAY MY SECOND GRADE TEACHER, Ms. Long, asked the class, "What do you want to be when you grow up?" Many around me yelled out, "A nurse!", "A football player!", "A cop!" *I'm not going to raise my hand. No one will understand my answer.* As I watched Ms. Long make her way to the chalk board, I shifted my focus back to the worksheet in front of me.

Before I could grab my pencil, she looked at me directly and stated, "Let's hear from Symbolie. What do you want to be when you grow up?" Filled with both fear of being teased and excited possibilities, I parted my lips and just above a whisper replied, "I want to be a mom!"

I AM THE ANCESTOR

Moms are loving
Moms are kind;
Moms are gentle
But, not mine.

Being a mom is absolutely everything to me! I still take pictures of my children on their first day of school and college. I realize the importance of investing in the lives of my children in order to help them develop into well rounded individuals who, I pray, will return the investment by making a tremendous impact on this world. So far, so good. The love, time, energy, and resources I pour into them produces structure, consistency, and a holistic way of life. My role as a mom is primary and extremely valuable. I often wonder what the changing face of my community would look like if every mother embraced her role this way.

I really enjoy sharing whatever I can with people in need. Never have I been the type of person to hoard my gifts because I understand that freely they were given to me so freely I must give to others. There are not many people who get this. They are so insecure and afraid that once they release something it will not come back to them. Giving is the only true way to receive.

On a daily basis, I see the need to get back to the basics of mothering. The newfound "Children First" philosophy with the United States Department of Education has never ceased to be my sermon. I live and breathe those words and the four children my Creator has blessed me with reap every possible benefit of that mantra. It is for this very reason that I began embarking on a way to help other young aspiring single mother's gain an understanding of the core principles needed for successful parenting. With the support of other women like them, it is really nothing they can not accomplish. Unfortunately, many still operate with a crab in the barrel mentality and, as a result, miss out on so many blessings. With that, I gave birth to what I consider "my masterpiece", my business: Cause I'm a Mom, LLC!

Some have told me, "Monique, you are much more than a mom!" That is very true. Please understand that the title of my business does not minimize my role. In fact, it speaks to the energy and drive that allows me to be so much more. You see, having this great title pushes me to be a successful business owner, a savvy investor, and a dedicated community activist. It keeps me going on those days when I want to stop and stops me on those days when I'm going too much. Sure, I'm much more than a mom. But it's because I'm a mom that I am so much more!

When I embraced this concept of providing services in this area, my wheels began to turn endlessly. I positioned myself to embark upon this race of establishing Cause I'm a Mom, LLC and every part of the business one step at a time. I was no stranger to business development. As the successful owner of a dump truck company, I knew what awaited me on the track. The feeling of entrepreneurial fitness over-whelmed me in the greatest of ways! I was ready! *Runners take your mark, get set...GO!*

The development of my brand and logo was in the first leg of my trek. I definitely wanted to paint a clear picture of my purpose and seriously capture the attention of every spec-tator. Cause I'm a Mom, LLC had to arrest the attention of every onlooker while sending the most captivating, heart-tugging message of "this is who I am and this is what I do". The significance of this company had to be easy to under-stand and the message needed to drive home the point that mothering is the job of all jobs! If a woman strives to be nothing else, she should strive to be a CEO Mom!

Once I completed that lap, I continued to trot and focused much time and energy towards developing the business structure and plan. My years of labor experience taught me to be "a committee of one" while affording others the opportunity to follow my lead. I boast of my strong work ethic and typically extend myself beyond the call of duty simply because I want to make a difference. I know the 80/20 rule—where 80% of the work is done by 20% of the people—will always be a factor, but I am determined to set trends and be of service to others. Again, it really puts me in a stronger receiving position.

My goal was to offer a variety of services and resources that were general in nature, such as preparing your child for college, but also unique to each mother's need and level of understanding. While we all have challenges, not all challenges are the same. I had to ensure I worked hard to captivate my audience, keep their attention, and make them hungry for more. I had to communicate to them on their level and take their individual needs into consideration. I researched other organizations in the community to get an idea of what was already out there and called a few just to share what I was attempting to do. For the most part, all were very helpful and answered many of my questions.

Moving right along, I decided that conducting weekly workshops on various topics that centered on being a mother would be a great place to start. A few of the topics I decided upon were:

- The unique struggles that a mother has to face.
- Raising a boy as single mother.
- Encouraging teenagers to practice safe sex without promoting and condoning children to have sex.
- Understanding the temperament of girls as they come of age and become independent.
- Teaching children to become sufficient by learning to cook and clean.
- Money generating ideas for children such as landscaping, basic household repairing, knitting, sewing, and crocheting,
- And one of my favorite topics that needed tackling:

What to do when you realize that you have a child who is gay

I was running this race to win! I began by developing a plan of action to outline both the human and material resources I would need. Next, I worked out my annual budget and plugged every possible number on an expense tracker with specific details outlining the return on my investment. I've learned long ago that the purpose of running a business is not only to serve the community, but to make money as well. When a product is produced or a service is provided, there is labor that goes into those tasks. Just as there are people who work for a paycheck at the end of the week, a business is operated for a defined period of time for a profit.

I revisited my research by locating specific parts of the community to see where the need was greatest. I went to schools, churches, community centers, shopping malls, libraries, and every possible grocery store sharing bits and pieces of my business idea. While I was there I was able to observe first hand the population of people at those locations. Let's just say everywhere I went in the community there was great potential to provide a service! Specifically with the private and faith based organizations I solicited as many stakeholders as I could with a common interest and was embraced by many.

Next, I began spreading the word through extensive community outreach and distribution of flyers. Because I was what some would call "the mom on the block" pitching my idea was really a breeze. The women were all but ready to come in my house and sit at my kitchen table. Finally, I secured both a written and verbal commitment from a community center and area school to host the workshop at their facilities. Within two months, I was ready! For all intents and purposes I was in business!

During this process, I contacted the Maryland Department of Assessment and Taxation to request the necessary applications and paperwork. I was determined to legitimize my business and not let it be a con, hustle, or "under the table" operation.. I totally believe in planning, preparing, and doing things the right way. The benefits are truly endless! My 40 plus years on this planet has taught me that there are serious consequences when I try to take short cuts. Eventually, you're left to go back and what should have been done from the beginning.

I understand and respect that systems are designed to create and maintain order and serve as a guide when developing just about anything.

About six weeks later, I received a letter from the State of Maryland Department of Assessment and Taxation. *Oh my gosh! This is it! This is it!* What I expected to be rather bulky in content was actually a standard envelope with a letter. My heart was beating rapidly and my hands were shaking with excitement as my thoughts side barred into awesome workshops, moms from all walks of life, and lots of hugs and tears because I've helped someone. *Cause I'm a Mom, LLC! What a difference I will make. What a difference.* I was on my way to finally realizing my dream of being in business. The chance I longed for to "officially" provide women with services that were necessary while hoping to touch their lives and share some of the love I have for mothering was here...in my hands. Emotions overwhelmed me. I was grateful, grateful, grateful!

Shaking with nervous anticipation, I grabbed my letter opener and proceeded to rip the envelope. *I think I'll start with the workshop on the meaning of being a mother. Maybe I should kick things off with a pot luck "Meet and Greet" just to break the ice.* My stomach began fluttering like butterflies on a beautiful spring day as vision upon vision resided in my mind. I placed my hand on the letter, slowly pulled it out, and opened it to find these words: REJECTED DUE TO INSUFFICIENT INFORMATION! NON-ESTABLISHED IDENTITY! I let out the most horrendous scream! "NO NOT AGAIN! GOD, NO!" It was 1996 all...over...again.

Congress had just enacted the Small Business Regulatory Fairness Act in 1996. One of its purposes was to create a more cooperative regulatory environment among agencies and small businesses that is less punitive and more solution-oriented. This was a great sign that becoming an entrepreneur was going to be beneficial. I enrolled in a class designed to teach the basics of developing a business management guide. Passing with outstanding marks, I received my certificate of completion and a great deal of information from the Small Business Administration on how to best establish my business. Immediately thereafter, I pursued other courses of entrepreneurship like filing a trade name, the purpose of the Federal Tax Identification number, establishing a business bank account, commercial realty, licensing and bonding, the benefits of business insurance and more. I was on a serious quest to learn all I could and left no table unturned. Focused and determined to do whatever it took to become a CEO, I acquired all the necessary certificates and submitted an application packet to the Maryland Department of Assessment and Taxation. Not more than four weeks later, the letter of rejection arrived in my mailbox because of my "NON-ESTABLISHED IDENTITY!"

My appetite for immediate answers consumed me! I longed to devour every possible bit of information to feed my famished soul. The unanswered questions in my clouded mind engulfed me like a raging sea abruptly tossing a steamboat to and fro. As my hands shook uncontrollably, I snatched my cell phone from its case and called the number at the bottom of the letter. My heart raced feverishly and my jumbled words ignored all grammatical rules. With great difficulty, I attempted to calm myself, speak slowly and clearly, and ward off the impending sea of tears as questions poured out of my trembling mouth.

I began to inquire about the rejection code and determine

the necessary action I should take to remedy it. The voice of the woman on the other end of the phone was slurred with extreme apathy. It was too obvious that she did not care one bit about my situation. Instead, protocol was the order of the day.

"Miss", she said dryly, "I can't give you any information about 'your' situation until you give me some adequate ID. You can be anybody on the other end of this phone!"

It was a Friday and the time was 4:43 p.m. *Oh my God! There is no way I'm going to make it across town in 17 minutes!* I had reached another dead end and that painful turn of events halted me from moving any further in the process.

It was not long thereafter that I decided to put my business pursuits on hold. Knots began forming in my stomach after colliding against so many brick walls. Literally for every step forward I took, I was knocked three steps back. The lack of identification was the prime hindrance. I was certain that until I got that matter rectified I would never be able to advance. The words "NON-ESTABLISHED IDENTITY" rode my brain like Evel Knievel on a customized Harley Davidson. Daunting thoughts raced around the track of my psyche with ease.

I began calling and sending letters to the Bureau of Vital Records, the Department of Social Services, and the Public School System to explain my unfortunate circumstance. I left no stone unturned as I relived the catastrophic blow to my pursuits. I had no doubt that these carefully scrutinizing government agencies would provide me with accurate answers as I sought to established myself for the powers that be. Since the law mandates that proper measures are executed when confirming a person's identity, I was, again, hopeful. *They will help me!*

Time passed swiftly. Within three weeks, I received two responses from two different agencies on the same day. Flashbacks of the rejection letters and fear of the unknown overwhelmed me. Both joy and pain etched out their respective spaces in the pit of my stomach Nervously, I decided to put those two letters aside and wait for the last response to come. "I'll just wait and open them all together", I justified out loud. Comforted by the thought, I shifted my attention to preparing my grocery list and clipping coupons.

To my surprise, the third correspondence arrived the very next day! I ran inside the house and immediately grabbed the other two letters off of my nightstand. I paused for moment as I looked at all three of them in my hand. I began to tremble and my palms became moist. *This is it!* Carefully, I tore open each envelope. *Maybe being gentle will give me the reply I'm looking for!* Sadly, my letter opener was met with one recurring disappointment after another as the pain vehemently evicted the crushed joy on the inside. In short, each agency replied that their investigation revealed inconsistencies with my date and place of birth. Furthermore, my social security number listed that I had three different names! *I am Symbolie Monique Smith! My name is SYMBOLIE MONIQUE SMITH! S-Y-M-B-O-L-I-E-M-O-N-I-Q-U-E-S-M-I-T-H!*

For years, I had questions about the events of my life but I was too afraid to ask. Mental scars as a result of physical pain trained me to keep my mouth shut.

> *When I asked*
>
> *If it's time to nap,*
>
> *Your harsh reply*
>
> *Was an aching slap!*

Numerous questions I formed about my life began to materialize right before my eyes. I suddenly had many questions.

What in the hell is going on? My mind began spiraling out of control! I was so very confused and did not know what to do. A surge of emotions brought me to my knees as I literally fell flat on my face. Rage, fear, and disappointment caused my heart to pound terribly. Instantly, I began to replay various scenes from my childhood:

- ► The time my cousin pulled me to the side and whispered, "I'm not really your cousin!"
- ► When I protested punishment because I was eighteen and my "mother" punched me in the face

repeatedly and said, "You're <u>not</u> eighteen...and I can prove it!"

► When my uncle brushed up against me in the most disgusting way and told me, "One day, you're going to be my woman!"

At that very moment it occurred to me that the woman that raised me for the past 30 years was obviously <u>not</u> my biological mother. Hindsight is always 20/20. We never shared a mother and daughter connection the way I have established with my daughters. We never went anywhere fun together. Throughout my entire life, this woman kept such a marked emotional distance; I have no recollection of ever being hugged, held, kissed, or affirmed. Whenever I looked at her, my eyes were met with the glare of venom. And when I spoke to her or tried to engage in a simple conversation with her, she would consistently retort, "What the fuck do you want?"

Disconnected and it felt so bad!

Disconnected you made me feel sad!

No love did you share...and you did not care,

A bond was never present cause were

Disconnected...hey, hey!

I gathered every piece of correspondence I received and

decided to take the necessary steps to pursue my past. As unpleasant and distressing as it was, I realized that in order for me to make sense of it I had to get answers. The uncertainties were too numerous to name and brought about so much agony, but that was not enough to prevent me from proceeding. In short, I had absolutely no choice! My sanity was depending on me to do something. It was the only way I was going to have any peace.

Before I beat the pavement to pay a visit to the government agencies that I was depending on to help me make sense of this madness, I made an attempt to get the answer from "the woman" who raised me. I didn't know what to expect, so I was a bit hesitant. One flashback after another of being beat or cursed out for asking simple questions stood as a warning to "PROCEED WITH CAUTION!" However, I pushed aside any concern for my welfare because I needed answers...by any means necessary!

I grabbed my phone and dialed her number in a hurry. I made no attempt to hide my emotion and I did not skate around the issue. *Gotta get answers! Gotta get answers!*

Finally, the ringing stopped and there she was on the other end of the phone. The temperature went from a toasty 79 degrees to 20 degrees below zero as she said, "Yeah? Hello?"

I greeted her back.

"What you want?" she asked.

"Mommy, I'm having trouble starting a business. I keep getting rejection letters that says my identity is not my identity. They keep saying I'm not really Symbolie Monique Smith and that I wasn't really born on May 13, 1966. I don't understand! This is not the first time this has happened to me," I said. "I've been trying for years and I keep getting the same rejection letters. What's going on, Mommy? Do you know?"

There was a brief pause and then profuse cursing.

"Who the fuck do you think you are calling me asking me some stupid shit like this? You still like playing those monkey ass games, Symbolie, don't you? Don't you? Look, don't be calling my house running up time on my phone with simple ass shit like this or I'll whip your ass some more! You ain't too old to get kicked in your damn face and I ain't too old to do it either. Now get the fuck off my damn phone and don't be calling me with your crazy shit!"

With an abrupt ringing in my ear from the phone being slammed in my ear, once again I was made to feel lower than the lowest.

It was time to hit the streets and seek out my own answers. This included talking to family and friends as well. I will discuss this in more detail later in the book. Day after day, week after week, and month after month I spent endless hours and money in pursuit of getting answers. I wrote countless letters, made tons of phone calls, and even took several trips to municipalities and states where I could possibly be linked.

I AM THE ANCESTOR

The results were the same: there was not a single piece of consistent information on who I was, when I was born, and where I was born. I felt defeated, but I did not give up!

To save money and stop losing time with my children, I started a mailing list. It included a total of ten pages of contact information for newspapers, clearinghouses, and other media outlets. I was fortunate that a few organizations reached out to me only to put a personal touch on another closed door of rejection. I became so consumed with trying to find my true identity that other areas of my life were being neglected. I began to recount the countless hours I spent away from my children, the money I invested, and even the state of my sanity. So, after several more months and dollars spent in getting answers, I decided to refocus for the betterment of my family!

It was very hard to swallow the fact that my life was halted. Being able to correctly identify myself was crucial to every area of my life! Because I could not "prove" who I was, I couldn't start a business, travel abroad, or even go back to school to get my college degrees. Basically, I couldn't attempt anything because typically a background check is required. Even as I write this book, I'm looking at an application that I need to complete to launch another business venture and it says, "BACKGROUND CHECK REQUIRED." I feel stuck. I am stuck and I am running out of time.

Recently while at my office, I decided to call the woman again who raised me. In short, she holds the key that will unlock my past, enhance my present, and propel my future in endless positive directions. My frustration was building and my emotions had a mind of their own! More than answers, I needed her to know what she was doing to me and how it had begun to impact my children. Although I was hoping for the best, I was totally prepared for the worst. It didn't matter to me what she said or how she said it. It was now my turn to speak my mind.

I snatched my phone from its case and swiftly dialed her number. No time for formalities. Honestly, I cared neither about the quality of her day nor her well-being. I needed answers to just one thing: why did my background check come back invalid...again? Before she even completely said, "Hello", I began speaking my mind.

"You are sixty eight years of age and you are not getting any younger! Everyone is either dead or dying around you and I honestly don't know how much longer you'll be around! Do you desire to ever tell me about my past? Are you ever going to tell me where you got me from? Am I to continue to live without the right to enjoy weekend get-a-ways with my girlfriends to the Bahamas or a nice cruise to the Mediterranean or a train ride to see Niagara Falls in Canada?"

She briefly got a word in edgewise. "What's...what's wrong? What are you talking about, Bolie? What's going on now?"

Ignoring her questions, I continued.

"Have you at least considered getting a safe deposit box at

the bank so you can put all of the information about me in it so that upon your death I would be notified of an envelope with a key and a lockbox? Do you have a safe in the house? Have you left any of this information with daddy? Does he even know the truth? Or do you truly desire to carry this to your grave? This is now affecting my children...your grand-children!"

All I heard was deep breathing in the background and Tammie sucking her teeth. Although she mumbled a few words, I could not make out what she was saying.

Her silence was only making me more furious to the point where I felt my stomach getting hot. When I have gotten to the point where I'm about to loose control, this is the feeling I get. Once I'm here, it takes a while for me to calm back down. I know it's best for me to not say anything to anyone while in this state because I just don't know what words will come out of my mouth. This time, I honestly did not care so I continued to speak.

"My son...your grandson...Christopher wants to attend a Shi Lin Temple in China," I continued. "He has been learning martial arts for several years now and has worked hard to get to the levels he's at. He told me close to two years ago that when he turned 16 years old, he wanted to fly to China and learn from the best. In order for him to go, he needs to have adequate parental consent including proper veri-fication of parental identity. Well, there's just one problem: I DON'T HAVE AN IDENTITY! In the event that he is even allowed to go over there and pursue his dream and something ungodly happens…like abduction or imprisonment or some hostage situation…what am I to do? Chinese authorities are not going to let me in their country no matter how much I tell them I'm his mother. I won't have the freedom to go over there to rescue him, support him, or aid him! How much more am I to suffer? I am 43 now…MAYBE…I don't know; but, you do! When are you going to stop holding onto the truth and tell me about how you got me?" I screamed.

Still, she said nothing. I could hear her turning off the television as her breathing got heavier. I went on.

"Mommy, I can't do anything! Nothing at all. Zero. What have I ever done to you for this to now roll over to affect my children? Do you know we last had this conversation 14 YEARS AGO and since then you've done absolutely nothing? You have done nothing but cause me an awful lot of grief and pain."

I felt myself calming down slowly but surely. With a little sarcasm, I continued.

"I'm assuming I shouldn't look to you to do anything now. I was never able to look to you for your help when I was a child, so why should I expect to look to you now. Your lack of actions speak very loudly and clearly and are beginning to answer some of the questions I've asked myself for years," I said.

"I no longer doubt whether or not you knew that I was being

molested and raped by two of your own brothers. I know you did. You actually gave me over to them for their pleasure anytime of the day or night. You had something to hide about me, but you could not hide it from them. So, to keep their mouths shut you used me as a bargaining chip. You prostituted me to them and in other ways all throughout my life. You knew, didn't you? You allowed them to have their way with me, Mommy. And what about the time I was in the hospital for close to three months? You lied and told the police that it was daddy who did that to me. That's why he never came to visit. You lied then, too, and told him I had a urinary tract infection and that he should not come around because the doctors and nurses were going to check on my throughout the day. But you know that I was in the hospital because your brother used me as his little sex toy from four years old to eighteen years old," I said crying.

"Remember the two by four? Well, I do! What child deserves to be beat like that? Have you ever been beat with a two by four? D o you know how that feels? Miss June knew about what you did. I showed her when you went to the bathroom the day you beat me with that piece of wood. Yeah. She knows all about how crazy you are," I said.

There was a very long pause. I was just waiting for her to slam the phone in my ear like she did in 1996. Instead, she stuttered and said, "I'm…I'm going to see. I know, I know. What do you want me to do? Oh, Lord, what did I do? I'm so sorry…sorry for this, Symbolie. I just don't remember what happened, but I'm going to do something. I'm going to do something."

"When? When are you going to do 'something'," I screamed. "I've always honored you and given you what-ever you needed. I've given you every proud mother and grandmother moment possible and still you won't help me," I said as my body ached from crying.

Her heavy breathing began to minimize as she continued to talk.

"I'm going to do something…I'll try…try," she said a bit con-vincingly.

"Do what?" I shot back.

"I'll go to New York," she said.

"Go to New York…when and where? Just tell me," I coun-tered.

The dialogue somewhat forced us both to calm down a bit. Besides, I was becoming exhausted from the emotional toll of the conversation with her. It was rough.

She then answered my question by saying, "I don't…don't kn…know."I felt defeated once again. This was the deadest of dead ends I've ever encountered and I knew I wasn't going to get the answers from her that I needed. I was ready to get off the phone. Before I hung up, I had just one more thing to say.

I AM THE ANCESTOR

"Since you don't remember the dates, Mommy, since you don't remember the time, and since you don't remember the people just do this for me: tell me if your were wearing a shirt that said, 'I NEED KIDS' or did you see someone in passing who said, 'I got kids…you want one?' Tell me what conversation went on for you to have even gotten your hands on me. Did you pick me up from a mall or a playground? Was I in a woman's stroller and when she turned her head you took me out of it? You have to tell me something," I pleaded.

"What's my name? Is it really Symbolie Monique Smith or is it something else? How did you come up with my name, Mommy? I have never heard of another person having the name that I have. Please, tell me something," I pleaded.

Briefly, there was silence. Then, she let out a very deep sigh and hung up the phone. That was the last time I spoke to her.

An entire hour and a half had passed from the minute I saw the application in my office until our conversation ended. As I began to regain my composure, I immediately became terrified. You see, I was actually driving in my car, but did not remember at what point I left my office. *Oh my gosh! How… when did I get in here? I was just at the office!* Completely engrossed in that moment, I hadn't realized that I had shut down my computer, locked my desk drawer, activated the telephone answering service and the alarm for the building, and got in my car. *Did I run a red light? Jesus, did I hit some-*

body while driving? Was I speeding? I could not remember a thing.

As I pulled up into the driveway of my home, I began wiping the tears from my eyes. My silk blouse was soaked and starting to stain. My mouth was extremely dry so I took a sip of my iced tea in the car which had become watery to the taste. Reaching for tissue from my glove compartment, I became startled and jumped back.

Over to my right was my son sitting in the passenger seat. *Christopher? When did he get here?* As if leaving my office unaware wasn't enough, I had even driven to pick my son up from school. I was completely baffled and trembling nervously. *I could not have driven this far and not know it. Oh my God!* At that very moment, I realized that he heard the entire conversation I had with that woman. That was the first time he heard my story.

I will never forget the look of confusion, hurt, sadness, and anger like never before on his face as he tried to make sense of what he just experienced. He knew his mother was hurting badly and because of that, he wanted to hurt someone in the worst way. Turning aside, I began to cry even more as I replayed bits and pieces of that heated conversation with the woman who raised me.

Quickly, I got myself together. My only thought now was how to save my son. I tried to figure out how to restore the image he had of his mother...if I could. *God, help me!* I could not form the right words to say to him. At the time, my head was spinning from the conversation with Tammie and from the look Christopher had on his face. I decided to get out of the car and go inside the house. Christopher had not moved by the time I opened the door. I was tempted to tell him to come into the house, but I could tell that he needed time alone. When I glanced back at him, he just sat there looking out the window.

I dropped my bags once inside and headed straight to the basement. It was still a little damp from the flood we recently experienced, but I did not let that stop me. In the closet were boxes with my important papers. One of those boxes contained documentation and photos collected over the years to help me piece my life together. They had gotten totally wet, but not beyond the point of recognition. Thankfully, they weren't destroyed.

Page by page, I began peeling them apart and putting them back in chronological order. My table and sofa were covered. Tears started falling once more as I looked at the picture of being in the hospital as a child. *It's alright, Monique. Keep going, you can do it.* I pulled up a smaller card table to place all of the index cards. I did not realize how much information I accumulated over the years.

Moments later, I heard the door open. When I looked, there was Christopher coming down the steps. He had obviously been crying. I did not say anything to him and he did not say anything to me. Instead, he walked over to the box, grabbed a few stacks of paper, and began peeling them apart with me. I became very emotional and paused what I was doing. Christopher put his arm around me and cried a bit, too. When we got ourselves together, we continued peeling those pages one at a time.

It became clear to me that if I died on that day Christopher would have been left with such horrible memories. There would be no one to tell any of my children who their mother really was. Christopher would have been left to draw whatever conclusions he could from what he overheard during our ride home. No one could have comforted him and convinced him of the truth.

So, I decided I must share my story! Honestly, what other choice did I have?

TWO

What if I die; My Children Must be Told

O VER THE NEXT FEW DAYS, I RELIVED THAT ENCOUN-
ter. What stood out the most was seeing the agony
on Christopher's face. It was as if he witnessed
someone ripping out my heart and throwing it away. In fact,
someone had: Tammie. Recurring dreams of the business
that I was pursuing inspired me. Alongside them were the
challenging thoughts and questions of ultimately sharing my
true identity with my children. It all really became too much
to bear.

As those thoughts sank in, I questioned the impact this
would have on them. Ever so cautious to protect their innocence, I determined to not let what I instilled in them to be
destroyed. I cherished our bond and would not let it be
destroyed by any means necessary. Courtney, Christopher,
Xavier, and Katlyn were valuable to me and respect my role
as their mother. Fighting to keep that all in tact was crucial.

Amidst this internal confusion, I still had to maintain our day to day routine. Life had to go on in a manner that would not cause any interruptions. I had worked too hard to develop the structure and balance in our lives for it to be destroyed. The way my children thanked me for that was by working just as hard at school. On the outside, I was keeping it together. On the inside, I was falling apart.

Several more days passed as I wrestled back and forth in my mind with what I knew ultimately had to be done. Question after question and scenarios too numerous to name greeted me when I woke up in the morning and lulled me to sleep at night. I kept telling myself that I could not chance the children hearing my story from someone else. All the torture, all the shame, and all the neglect had to be told by me. How I tell them, when I tell them, and how much I tell them were the main questions.

Arriving home from work one day, I decided to call a family meeting. My daughter Katlyn met me at the door with her usual, "Hello, Mommy" and a big hug. I held her tightly and a little longer this time. As we released each other, she looked at me somewhat strangely and asked, "Are you OK, Mommy?"

Her question was very serious. Katlyn never likes to see me sad or upset. It causes the same feelings in her. As I looked at her round little face, I recalled the look on my son's face just a few days before. The contrast caused a lump to form in my throat. I was not OK, but I could not let her know that. More questions would have been asked and I'm sure my tears would have flowed. Katlyn is that type of child. She is very inquisitive and has a need to get to the bottom of things.

I replied, "Oh, nothing. I'm just really glad to see you, Katlyn!"

With the picture of both Christopher's face from a few days ago and now Katlyn's face, I asked myself, "Why would I leave the burden on him or my oldest child to relay who his mother was to their younger siblings?" That alone forced me to buckle down and call a family meeting.

For the past ten years on every first day of the month, I've held a family meeting. This time, however, it was the middle of them month. While gathering the family together was going to be effortless and while it was not unusual for me to call an additional family meeting, I knew my request was going to raise a red flag.

When everyone arrived, they went to their usual spot on the sofa and floor in the living room with comfort food in hand. Christopher was silent. He appeared to have much on his mind. In part, I believe he had an idea of what was going to take place at the meeting. The other three children, however, began firing away.

"It's not the first of the month, Mom," Xavier said.

"Did someone do something wrong?" Katlyn asked with serious concern.

Courtney chimed in. "You're not having another baby, Mom...are you?"

Chatter amongst them continued as they tried to figure out if we were going to have a debate, plan our family vacation, or welcome a new addition to the family. All the while I was silent which further heightened their curiosity. As I listened to the sound of each of their voices, my heart became very heavy. All I could think of is how much I love my children and how grateful I am to be their mother.

With four different age groups present, I wanted to make this as easy as possible. Capturing their attention in a manner that they could all understand was going to take a bit of creativity. It appeared the best approach to take was to begin with explaining the meaning of a family tree. So I invited each of them to join me at the bay window in the dining room and then I began to share.

"You see that tree right there," I looked to Katlyn and asked as I pointed.

"You mean the only tree in the front yard, Mom? Yeah, I see it," she said. "It's getting big, isn't it?"

Rubbing her arm with a smile, I said, "It sure is. Just like all of you."

"Is something wrong with the tree?" Xavier asked.

I shook my head no and continued to speak. "That is what

people normally call 'a family tree'. Each branch represents a different generation of people in the same family."

They all appeared to understand what I was saying so I continued.

"See the big branch? Well, that would be considered the grandmother or grandfather family tree member. Now, you see the smaller branches? That's like the mother and father family tree member. And when you look a little closer, you'll see the even smaller branches or twigs and those are the children family tree members."

Both Courtney and Christopher looked somewhat somber yet relieved. Over the years and when I felt they would understand, they learned bits and pieces of my past. This, of course, gave them an advantage over Xavier and Katlyn who knew nothing at all. I could tell Courtney and Christopher were starting to understand where I was going with the talk because I always told them that the day would come when I would share more details. Today was the day.

One by one the questions came flooding in from Xavier and Katlyn. Courtney and Christopher looked on.

"How come you don't have a sister?" Xavier asked.

Before I had a chance to answer, Katlyn chimed in.

"Yeah! How come grandma only had you? Didn't she want more children so you would have someone to play with?"

"Where is everybody at, Mom?" Xavier asked perplexed. "Did they all die or something?"

"Mommy, why don't we have family reunions and stuff like my friends at school? They always talk about going to Myrtle Beach or Virginia to be with their family for two or three days. We should do that one day, Mommy," Katyln said somewhat pitifully.

Without saying a word, I walked over to a flower pot, placed my left hand deep in the soil, and scooped up a handful.

Christopher, who typically thinks before he speaks, blurted out, "What are you doing, Mom?"

I paused for a moment as the tears began to form in my eyes. The flashback of that look on his face wrenched my heart once more. *Now is the time. I can not leave him and Courtney to try and help my babies understand.*

My hands began to tremble slightly as I walked over to the bay window where my beautiful plants were. I reached over and snapped off four leaves, placed it into the soil in my left hand and said, "This plant was once a very tiny seed. As it grew, it became connected to other plants in the same pot or the same plant family. But one day, someone broke off a piece of the plant, moved it away from its plant family, and placed it into a different pot where it had to start growing all over again."

Katlyn had a look of both intrigue and pity. "Why would

someone break off a piece of the plant, Mommy? Didn't they know that would hurt the plant and make it feel alone?"

Nearly overcome with emotion, I forced myself to speak. "Children, Mommy is like this broken plant. There are no family roots, no family tree for me. Like this plant in my hand, I have no connection to my family or my past. For Mommy, you are the branches that are growing from my seed. It all begins with me and continues with you."

Xavier blurted out, "That's impossible! You can't be the seed, Mommy. You had to come from somewhere."

With both relief and sadness, I simply said, "Baby, this is why I called this meeting today."

I could tell that my children felt the seriousness of the meeting. All eyes were on me as silence totally fell over the room. By now, they knew the meeting had nothing to do with vacations or babies but everything to do with me. They shifted their position to find a more comfortable spot. I placed the soil and plant in a small pot, grabbed a couple of wet napkin from off of the table to clean my hands, and continued to speak.

"The time has come in our lives where I've taken us as far as I can. My past is now hindering your ability to maximize your potential to its fullest extent. Mommy has always focused on providing the best possible life for you. I have established a mini-empire to leave as a legacy for each of you."

I paused briefly as my mind took me back to each of their first: first steps, first teeth, first boo-boo, and first day of school. Overcome with emotions, I dropped my head into the palms of my hands and cried uncontrollably. Like clockwork, Courtney and Christopher moved from the couch and sat next to me, one on each side. Courtney rubbed my arms and Christopher put his arms around my shoulder.

"Don't cry, Mommy," Katlyn said as she began crying herself.

Tears began streaming down Xavier's face, but he wiped each one before it met his cheek. Without saying a word, he got up, walked into the bathroom, grabbed the box of tissue, and gave it to me. Mustering up a little strength, I continued to speak.

"If I do not share my past with you, children, it could possibly bring about more damage to us all. If there were another way to do what I know must be done without any complication, I would jump on right away. Because no one really knows the truth the way I do, I can not take the chance of you learning about your mother from anyone else. I don't want any family members speaking of me in sympathetic tones that will only leave you trying to figure out what they meant," I said.

A lump began to rise in my throat once more. This time, I forced it to stay in its place and continued to speak.

"What I'm about to share with you is very saddening and

painful. I know that it will make you feel the same way. I've made it my life's mission to shield you from anything that would bring you harm or disrupt our home because I love you so much. I know that life has its ups and downs, but the thought of any of you experiencing any pain is unbearable. However, I have no choice but to do what I'm about to do."

I extended my hands and gestured that each of them come closer to me. I wanted to put my arms around them so they could truly feel my love. I found myself right in the middle of them as they flung over my back, hugged my waist, lay on my lap, or held my hand. Loosing all self-control, I cried much harder. My children cried as well. *You can do this, Monique. Breathe and pull yourself together.*

"Children, I hope and pray that the times we have spent together as a family and the trust we've worked so hard to build will not be destroyed by anything I reveal to you in this meeting," I said through a halted voice. "The mere thought of ruining my relationship with any of you tears my heart apart. Please know that I've given careful thought to how I should go about this. You may not be able to handle some of what I'm about to share and it may even be alarming to you. However, what's most important is that you receive all the facts about the identity of your mother."

Composing myself more, I wiped away tears and continued.

"I do not wish to leave you on this earth without me being

the one to tell you first, just as I've done with everything else. I was the first one to tell you about the boogie man and the first one to tell you that Santa Claus, the Easter Bunny, and the Tooth Fairy were all make believe."

By this time, all the children were rather calm. After a few sniffles more, we all regained ourselves. Then, I made my final statement.

"I'm going to take you back to my very first memory of life. Some of the things that you are going to hear...please do not allow it to change the relationship that we have build. That's a big thing to me. Baby, There is no one that will ever be able to gift this information to you. There are no aunts, uncles, cousins, or great grand parents who know the truth about me the way I do. If Mommy does not tell you my beginning, then your end will be greatly impacted. This is why I must tell you my story...before I die."

THREE

My History Begins with Pain; The Story Begins

SATURDAY MORNING HAD FINALLY ARRIVED! I KNEW MY favorite day of the week was going to be filled with morning cartoons and, hopefully, a chance to play with my baby doll...by myself. I named her Sugar because she was so sweet to me. I usually got up early so I could be alone in the living room for as long as I could. It gets a bit crowded at times living in my grandmother's house with up to eight people at times. There was me, my mom, three of my uncles, my grandmother, and my grandfather.

My grandfather was actually a minister. He was about 30 years old when he married my grandmother. She was only 12 at the time. The marriage was forced because my grandmother got pregnant. This was round about 1938 or so. Back in that day, that's just how it was. I never heard any of my family say anything negative about their father.

So not to disturb anyone, I quietly walked down stairs,

turned on the television, and sat on the couch with Sugar. For about a good half hour I was all alone. It was a very peaceful moment that I recall to this day. As I sat holding Sugar, I began to pretend that I was a real mommy. Gently I brushed her hair and slicked it down with a bit of saliva on my finger. As she sat on my lap, I whispered, "Mommy loves you and will always love you, Baby." I raised her to my face, looked her in her eyes, and winked to reassure her of my love. I then gave her a big hug as I patted her back. Crazy as it may seem, I felt her love in return.

Just then, I heard someone coming down the stairs. I immediately placed Sugar on the couch next to me and looked directly at the television. *If I don't move maybe no one will see me.* Out the corner of my eye I could see that it was Tammie. I could tell by the cartoon I was watching that it was not quite nine o'clock in the morning. It was rare for Tammie to be up before 11 a.m. Normally she slept late on Saturday's because due to all the partying she would do Friday night. But to my surprise, she was dressed, and ready to leave out the house.

My curiosity got the best of me. As interesting as those cartoons were, I couldn't help but wonder what caused Tammie to rise so early. Innocently I asked, "Where are you going Mommy?" as I picked up Sugar and placed her on my lap once more. What came next was the beginning of a very painful lesson for me to learn at the tender age of five.

Tammie reached over the back of the couch, snatched

my baby from my lap and said, "Who the fuck is the adult, Bolie?" as she slapped me on the back of my neck. My neck felt like it was on fire; the sting was unlike anything I had ever felt before. Frightened, I crawled to the corner of the couch, gathered my legs to my chest, dropped my head on my knees, and closed my eyes real tight. All I heard were footsteps on those hardwood floors. I hoped she would walk out the door at that point. Instead, she made her way to the front of the couch.

Grabbing me by my wrists, she yanked me off of the couch and forced me to stand up and look at her. I could not see her very well because my eyes were full of tears. Every time I tried to wipe them, she would move my hands from my face. Tammie was furious at this point. I knew this meant more of the same…or worse…was on the way.

Another slap came. This time it was on my back. "Who is the goddamn adult in this goddamn house?", she screamed.

With another slap, this time to my face, she went on. "Who do you think you are asking me where am I going? I'm a grown woman, Bolie. Shit, Girl! You don't have the right to ask me a goddamn thing," she yelled as she talked with her teeth.

I tried to back up because I could see that she was going to hit me again. My eyes became fixated on her black leather belt with that iron looking buckle. All I could think was I hope she don't take off her belt. As I looked to my right, I saw Sugar on the floor. When Tammie threw her, she landed in an upright position with both hands raised in the air. I will never forget that because in my five year old mind my "baby" was trying to tell me to come pick her up from off the floor. *Mommy's coming, Sugar. I'm coming. Somebody help me!*

My few steps in the other direction really made her mad! *Just stand still, Symbolie.* She jumped directly in front of me and I froze. "Mommy," I pleaded, "I'm sorry! Please, Mommy! I won't do it again." I realized that nothing I said or did would stop Tammie at this point. Her agenda was clear: to beat me until I met the floor. I knew I was just going to have to ride this whipping out and deal with the pain later.

"What the hell do you mean asking me 'Where you going, Mommy?'" she asked.

With her fingers pointing in my face and a slap, push, or punch between words, she continued.

"Don't you ever question me like that again in your life, do you hear me, Girl?" she demanded.

I screamed, "Mommy! Mommy!" as several more hits came before she finally knocked me into the sofa and then pushed me on the floor.

I landed on my face. All I could do was cry as I lay on that cold hardwood floor. The pain from the punches and slaps remained for what seemed like hours. I tried to move twice but my body was burning as if one hundred queen bees hooked their stingers inside of me. The more I cried, the more my little body jerked. This only caused more pain so I began to take deep breaths to help me stop. After I settled down, I managed to turn my head to the side and rest it on my arms as they overlapped each other.

The crying made me very tired so I decided to just stay on the floor. Feeling the urge to sleep, I allowed myself to drift off for a moment. My mind began to replay what just happened and it caused me to cry again. *What did I do? Why did Mommy do this to me? I don't understand.* The tears welled up in my eyes once more and slowly ran from one eye to the next and then down one side of my cheek. I reopened my eyes for a moment and then began drifting off to sleep again.

I was startled awake when Tammie screamed, "Get your ass up!"

Before I had a chance to move, she grabbed me by my leg, slid me closer to her, and then yanked me up by my arm.

"Since you think you can ask me questions, go to your fucking room, stay there until I say you can come out, and think about how you can learn to not ask me any stupid questions. I am the adult and you are the child and if you know what's good for you, you will stay in a child's place", she shouted as she led me with a jerk to the stairs.

I climbed up to my bedroom as quickly as my throbbing body could carry me. My legs felt like they were about to fall off as I climbed each step. Finally reaching my door, I entered my room and closed the door quietly. If she even thought I slammed the door, she would have beaten me again. I stood still for a moment as brief flashbacks of what just occurred ran through my mind. I felt very numb as I cried without making a noise. Confused, sad, and lonely, I climbed on my bed to lie down.

A few moments later, I heard her yell, "I'm gone, Horace." Before he had a chance to respond, I could hear the familiar squeak of the front door opening and shutting. I let out a big sigh of relief. *She's gone.* I felt free. After that experience, I never thought of questioning her again.

It was getting close to the afternoon, so I decided to get dressed. I knew that the house would be bursting at the seams in a little while. On most weekends, my grandmother would make a little extra money by babysitting my cousins and other children in the neighborhood. I would often play with them when I could. Tammie generally found a reason to punish me. "Stay in your room" was an expression I heard often. I never really did anything. I just think she felt I did not deserve to have any fun.

On this particular weekend there were about twelve children left with my grandmother. With my Uncle Horace there, too, she did not have too supervise us too closely. He was known for teaming us all up for one type of game or another. I could hear them shouting, "Me, me!" from my bedroom as I sat there imagining all of the fun they were going to have. Then, I heard them go out the front door. I ran to the window in time to see them lining up on the side-walk for a race.

I wish I could run
Straight to the sun.
One day real soon;
My time will come.

It did not take Uncle Horace long to notice that I was not in the crowd of children. Immediately, he came to my room, knocked on my door, and called out, "Bolie? You in there?" One of the reasons I really loved my Uncle Horace is because he never just walked into my room. He always knocked first. Out of everyone in my family, I really felt that he loved me and wanted the best for me.

I was really afraid to answer the door but the sounds of laughter and screaming from the other children outside made me want to pull it open. When he knocked on the door a second time, I slowly turned the knob, cracked open the door, and ran back to my bed. When he entered, he was able to see that I had been crying. I saw on his face that he knew what happened. He knew that Tammie had a field day on me as he gently touched the bruise on my head. The look on his face was one of both anger and pity.

"Come outside with me so you can play a game with the others. We're about to have a race and it's going to be fun", he said with as much excitement as he could. I began to cry as I tried to explain to him what happened and what Tammie would do to me if I left the room. I was clearly very afraid to move from that bedroom, but he did not listen. Instead, he reached for my hand and said, "I'll protect you. Plus she'll never know that you left the bedroom because I'll have you back up here before she gets home.

I felt safe and believed every word he said. Even though I was still very afraid and my skin tightened with the thought of being beat like that again, I put my hand in his and he lead me out of my bedroom.

My cousins and other children from the neighborhood greeted me with the usual, "Hey, Bolie" as I stepped outside the front door. One of my cousins looked me up and down and then said, "What's wrong with you? You look like you been crying again." I didn't say anything because she already knew why I had been crying. Everybody knew.

Uncle Horace told me to take a seat on the porch with the other children. He announced that we were going to have a race and began forming the teams. It was really nice to be outside for a change. While most children were shouting for certain children to be on their team, all I cared about was racing against the other children and having lots of fun.

I AM THE ANCESTOR

It was always fun to watch Uncle Horace when the children would race against each other. He got really excited as we zoomed past him running at top speed. I guess we reminded him of his favorite pastime: night car races. You could always hear him get ready for his "game" with his car. I didn't quite understand why anyone would race in the dark. It seemed to me that it would be more of an accident than a race.

The game lasted well into the afternoon. I felt like I had been running up and down the side walk for hours. I was having the best time playing outside. It took my mind off of the pain I felt earlier that morning.

It was now time for the final lap we called "The Big Race." I never lost "The Big Race" because I was really fast. We were all lined up across the sidewalk. I learned a long time ago to position myself on the outside of the line. This kid strategy kept me from being bumped like the other children who were in the middle of the line and it helped me to win.

First, Uncle Horace stood right in the middle of the line. This way, he could see if we were starting at the same place. He would look from left to right and left again. Once he determined that we all had our foot on the same line he would say, "On your mark, get ready, get set…GO!"

I took off running as fast as I could. I raced past one car and then the next car and then the bus stop. I was moving at top speed; I was running the fastest I think I ever ran. *Yes!*

I'm going to be the winner. That'll give them something to talk about!

It was the final stretch of the race and I was ahead of the other children by at least two cars. Winning by a landslide was in my future...or so I thought. Just as I was about to reach the finish line, I lost my footing on an extremely narrow portion of the sidewalk. I began to stumble. As my body leaned forward, I could feel gravity pulling me downward. My unsuccessful attempt to raise my head was met head on with a fire hydrant. I tripped over my feet, tumbled to the ground, and rolled about the distance of one car down the sidewalk.

When I stopped rolling, I stood up immediately. All the pain that resulted from being beat by Tammie was now joined by open wounds and lots of blood. As I looked around, all of the children were laughing at my unfortunate crash landing. Not one of them checked to see if I was hurt or needed any help. In fact, they decided to have the race again and started to pick teams. I began to cry uncontrollably just as Uncle Horace came to my aid. When I looked at his face, it was the same look of sadness and helplessness that I saw earlier that day.

"Tell me where you are hurt, Bolie," he said as he began to gently brush the dirt off my hands and face.

I responded by pointing to my knee and the right side of my face. Uncle Horace inspected those areas as I checked out my arms and stomach. I began to feel a burning sensation on my shoulder and realized my clothes were torn. A small patch of skin was missing to the point where I saw the white of my flesh.

After Uncle Horace finished dusting me off, he gave me a very long hug. "I'm sorry, Sweetie," he said as he grabbed me by my hand. It seemed as if he felt defeated. Almost as if he lost the race as well. "Come on. Let's go back into the house," he sighed. Once inside, he took me back upstairs to my bedroom and left me there...alone.

I sat on the edge of my bed and began to cry. I knew any moment Tammie would be back and the evidence that I had been outside would greet her with a resounding, "Hello!" The hard crying and fear of being beat again caused my little body to shake. There was nothing that I could say or do to avoid her punishing wrath. Terrified, I just waited.

I must have been in my bed room for about 15 minutes when I heard the front door open and slam shut. Tammie was back and she was in a rage. Apparently she met the children on the sidewalk and they told her the tale of "The Big Race."

"Horace? Horace? Where the fuck are you? I know your big ass is around here somewhere," she screamed to the top of her lungs.

I heard Uncle Horace talking to her in his usual even voice, but with firmness. This was the way he typically handled arguments with Tammie. No matter how ugly she became, he remained very consistent. He knew how she was...we all knew, in fact...and being ugly in return was not going to get results.

Tammie must have called him every name in the book. Threats about what she was going to do to him and to me slid out of her mouth effortlessly.

"What the hell was she doing outside anyway?" she asked. "I told her to stay in her room and think. But, you decided to stop her from thinking, took her outside, and let her get all dirty and shit? Who do you think you are, mother fucker?" she said.

Uncle Horace was not backing down. "It ain't right, Tammie, for you to treat that child that way! You always send her to her room for silly shit. The poor girl asked you a simple question and you beat her like she stole something," he said.

"You just plain crazy, Tammie, and you need to get help before you do something really crazy one day, " he continued.

I heard footsteps making their way upstairs. I knew it was Tammie. Then, I heard Tammie scream, "Get your mother fucking hands off of me Horace? Let my damn arm go!"

Uncle Horace screamed, "Don't you touch that child. I'm telling you, don't touch her," he firmly said.

"Don't nobody tell me what to do with my damn child. You

better get your hands off of me before I fucking beat your ass too, Horace. You know I ain't scared of you," she said.

"I'm outta here, you crazy bitch," he yelled. Then I heard the door slam. Uncle Horace left the house and did not come back for the rest of the day.

I sat on my bed frightened at the thought of what was about to happen. I was hoping that she was not coming for me this time. Maybe, just maybe, she would go to her bedroom, calm down, and then talk to me about the importance of obeying. Perhaps this time she would teach me a lesson by using words and not through a whooping. I was a smart little girl and would have gotten the message just as clear if she had talked to me.

My wishful thinking was interrupted moments later when Tammie came bursting through my bedroom door. My eyes immediately locked in on her hand and noticed that she was holding a black belt with a huge silver looking buckle. I had been beat by many belts but I had never seen that one before. She may have bought it while she was out shopping earlier that day. I believe she bought it just to whip me.

"Who the fuck told you to leave this bedroom, Bolie? Huh? Answer me, bitch!" she yelled as she shook me back and forth.

"Now look at you! You got your clothes all dirty and shit and that means I gotta wash them because you slipped outside behind my damn back when you know your ass was supposed to stay in this room," she said

"I did what you said, Mommy. I stayed in my room," I pleaded.

"Uncle Horace came and got me and told me to go play with the other children and I told him that I could not leave the room but he grabbed my hand and took me outside with the other children and he made us all race and I learned what you said, Mommy! I'm not going to question you and talk back and I'll be good I promise, Mommy, I promise," I said while crying uncontrollably.

Then, Tammie spoke two familiar words. "Come her." At that point, it was clear to me that I was about to endure yet another beating. Nothing I could say would have saved me from that.

As I slowly moved towards her, I wiped my eyes and just above a whisper begged one last time, "Please, Mommy. Don't beat me."

It did not work.

In her fury, Tammy grabbed the belt and she started swinging in every direction. That belt hit me on my legs, side, arms, and back. I screamed and hollered in agony. But, that did not matter to Tammie. She wanted to make sure I knew to never do that again. After that experience, I knew.

The beating did not last as long as the last one, but there

was lots of blood left on my clothes. It must have come from my skinned knees and the scar on my back, elbows, and the palms of my hands that I got from falling during the race. When Tammie beat me the way she did, the open wounds couldn't help but bleed.

My wounded flesh was throbbing. I felt cold, even though it was a very warm day, and very tired. It was still very early in the day, but Tammie sent me to bed. She didn't even have the decency to clean me up first. There I was – dirty, bloody, motionless, and scared out of my mind. No one came to comfort me or to see if I was dead or alive. There is no greater agony than to feel down on yourself and all alone. For the rest of the evening I didn't hear my uncle or the children. All I heard was the tears from my eyes hitting my pillow. *Why, God? What did I do?* Then, I drifted off to sleep.

The next day, I took my time getting out of the bed. I was in no rush to leave the bedroom fearing that one wrong move would land me another beating. My body was stiff and very, very sore. The throbbing was not as bad as before and the bleeding had stopped. I walked as fast as I could to the bathroom to take a bath. As I ran the warm water, I could only imagine the stinging that I would feel. Water on open wounds is not fun. For a moment, I actually thought of just going down stairs in my dirty, bloody clothes. *Nobody will care anyway.* Quickly dismissing that idea, I got in the tub, rinsed my body off with as much water as I could toler-ate, and got out. I wasn't about to put soap on my arms and legs and a towel was out of the question. I decided to let my tiny little body air dry.

After getting dressed, I had no choice but to face the day. There were many voices coming from downstairs so I figured it was safe to join them. Tammie rarely hit me in front of other people. When she did, it was not as severe as her private beatings. Slowly, I opened my bedroom door and began making my way downstairs. The first person I noticed was my grandmother. Then, I noticed a few of the other adults in my family. They all looked at me very pitifully. They were clearly able to see the bruises on my face and arms. I looked around for Uncle Horace, but he was not there.

I made it a point to act with caution from that point forward. I wondered about what to do and what to say or if I should do or say anything at all. With her, anything would justify me getting another beating. I did my very best to stay busy sweeping the floor or doing another household chore that would remove me from her presence. I made sure to do this up until she left the house for the day. It would have been nice to stay with someone else at their house. But, that never happened.

****

One of the family members that I grew up with was my Aunt Shelly. She was mentally challenged and probably about ten years older than me. Aunt Shelly was the youngest of my grandmother's children. Throughout my life, I shared a bed-room with her. Tammie took the liberty to beat her, too, for no reason at all. Aunt Shelly was not a threat to anyone and I never witnessed her doing anything other than staying real close to my grandmother. I guess that's what made Tammie so angry. She may even have been jealous.

When I was about six or seven years old, Tammie had a boyfriend named Cedric. They spent a great deal of time together. He was famous for bringing her treats and other gifts. He also bought treats for my grandmother like soda pop and ice cream. Cedric was very respectable and made sure that he addressed my grandmother as "Ma'am." Tammie really liked him and it appeared that he really liked her, too. Whenever he would come to the house, Tammie acted like the sweetest person in the world towards me and everyone else around her. *I wish you could move in with us, Cedric.*

On one of his visits, he asked Tammie if he could take me and Aunt Shelly to the drive-in movie.

"They are always stuck up in this house, Tam. Let me take them out for some fun for a while. When I come back, you and I can hang out at the bar, OK?" he said quite convinc-ingly.

To my most pleasant surprise, Tammie agreed. She told me and Aunt Shelly to go wash our faces and grab a jacket because it was a bit chilly that afternoon. We did as she said and then made our way out the door with Cedric.

I was too excited! This was one of those rare occasions that I got a chance to go someplace fun. Going outside of the house without Tammie was fun all by itself. I felt really happy for Aunt Shelly, too. She and I were truly the caged birds in the family. Because they were embarrassed by her disability, aside from her routine doctor visits, she never went further than our front step. In fact, they made her stay at the kitchen table most of the time. This way, they cold keep an eye on her.

It did not take us long to get to the movies. Just as we were turning into the lot, I saw that the movie we were going to see was "Charlotte's Web." I did not know much about it, but recalled some of the children in my classroom talk about their favorite parts. All I knew was that there was a nice pig, a mean rat, and a beautiful spider name Charlotte who died in the end. *I wonder if she was beat to death.* In a moment, I was going to find out for myself.

After paying the admission, Cedric parked way in the back. I thought that to be quite strange considering there were not many people out that day. The lot was practically empty. *He should park in the front. They have plenty of space up there.* For a minute I thought of asking him if we could move closer, but I was too afraid to open my mouth. I just kept quiet and prepared myself for the fun I was going to have.

We got to the drive-in just as the movie was about to start. Not wasting any time, Cedric attached the speaker to his side of the car, and reclined his seat. I was getting comfortable, too. With Aunt Shelly in the seat next to him, I had the entire back seat to myself.

Just as I was about to kick off my tennis shoes, Cedric turned to me and said, "Here, Bolie. I'm giving you five dollars. Go to the snack bar and bring us back three bags of popcorn and three soda pops. If there is any change left, you can keep it for yourself, OK?"

I was happy as a lark! *Popcorn, soda, and I can keep the change? Wow!* Without hesitation, I took the money and made my way to the snack bar. Because of where Cedric parked, I knew it was going to take me a while to get there and back. But I didn't mind at all. I was free for a moment from Tammie, I was at the movies with two people that I knew would not beat me or curse at me, and I was about to get some hot buttery popcorn, soda pop, and change! What more could a little girl ask for?

Making my way back to the car, I would stop along the way and watch bits and pieces of the movie. I wanted to make sure I didn't miss a single scene. That way, when I got back to school, I could join in the conversation with the other children and show them just how much I knew about the movie, too.

I was just a few steps away from the car. All of the goodies were in hand as I readied myself to jump in the back seat and really enjoy the movie. Because the speaker was on the driver side of the car, I decided to enter on the passenger side. As I went around the car, I did not see Aunt Shelly or Cedric. For a minute, I was scared. I thought they had left me at the movies by myself. To keep from crying, I told myself that they would be back for me soon.

When I finally got to the door, I realized that they were still in the car. I was relieved. As I was making my way back inside, I saw Aunt Shelly's skirt up to her waist and her panties down at her knees. Cedric was leaning over her with his face in her neck, hand between her legs, and his penis out of his pants. He did not notice that I had returned to the car, so he kept doing what he was doing. Thinking nothing of it at the time, I grabbed the door handle and tried to get back in the car.

Shocked that I was there, Cedric looked at me and yelled, "Go back to the concession stand for candy, OK? Just use the money left in your hand and I'll give you some more later!"

I left the car again, but this time I did not take as long to get back. I was very anxious to get in the back seat and really enjoy the movie. When I finally got back, Cedric and Aunt Shelly were sitting up again. I made my way to the back seat, kicked off my tennis shoes, ate my popcorn and candy, and watched the movie. What a fun time I had that day!

A few months had passed since seeing "Charlotte's Web", but I still remembered every single part. It was a very long time before I went back to another drive-in movie.

I AM THE ANCESTOR

While in the kitchen getting a cup of water, my grand-mother called me to her bedroom. Approaching the door, I heard Aunt Shelly crying and saying, "No...no..." and Tammie screaming at her. I had no idea what was going on, but I could tell that it was pretty bad.

I knocked on the door and was told to enter. They were all sitting on the bed at the time. Aunt Shelly had her head down and my grandmother was crying. Tammie, on the other hand, had a scowl on her face that I knew all too well. That piercing look went right through me and froze me in my tracks. I became frightened because I knew I was going to get beat for something...or nothing at all. As my grand-mother sat there quietly, Tammie began asking me a series of questions very calmly.

"Remember when Cedric took you and Shelly to the movies?" she asked.

I nodded my head to say, "Yes."

"Where did y'all go, Bolie? What movie did you see? Where were you sitting in the car? Is that the only place you went?" Tammie asked, back to back.

I answered Tammie honestly and innocently. Her questions seemed harmless so I figured that maybe she wanted to know about "Charlotte's Web", too. In spite of that, I still could tell that something just was not right.

Then, it dawned on me that something was terribly wrong

when she asked me, "Did you see anything strange at the movies with Shelly and Cedric, Bolie?"

I looked at Shelly and noticed that she was rocking back and forth and my grandmother was trying to hold her still. She only behaved this way when she was upset about something.

Tammie went on to ask, "Did anything strange happen?"

Without childlike eyes and no hesitation, I said, "Yes! When I got back to the car with the popcorn and soda, I saw Aunty's skirt up and her panties down. Aunty was laying back and and Ce..."

Before I could finish saying his name, Tammie looked at me and said, "Your ass is mine now, Bolie."

I looked at my grandmother who was crying uncontrollably. She could not see my silent plea for help because she was too consumed with her own grief and Shelly's as well, who kept rocking back and forth. *Please, Grandma! Please help me!*

Tammie was furious!

"You couldn't tell me? Huh? Why didn't you say something, Bolie? Here it is three damn months later and you decide to say something now. Shit...shit...shit! Fuck it. I'm going to kick your little yellow ass," she yelled.

My grandmother pulled herself together a bit and screamed,

"It's not her fault, Tam. Don't beat that child for something she ain't done. She ain't do it, Tam. She's only a little girl that don't know nothing about nothing. That man of yours did this. He's the one that deserves to be beat!"

It was that last statement that made Tammie look at my grandmother and say, "Shut up!"

Holding onto Shelly as tights as she could, my grandmother said, "Leave Bolie alone, Tam. That chile' ain't did nothing wrong. It ain't her fault. We can just get Shelly an abortion, that's all. Leave Bolie alone!"

Although Shelly was not very smart, she knew that "abortion" was not a good thing. I had no idea what it meant, either. At the top of her lungs, she started to yell, "No!" The screech was ear piercing.

Before I knew it, Tammie grabbed me and began to wail on my little body with her belt.

"Why didn't you tell me they were doing that shit? You don't think I need to know? Why the fuck did you let this shit happen, Girl?" she demanded as she cried and yelled.

The beating was short but painful. Tammie's emotions really got the best of her. She slammed down her belt, grabbed me by the shoulder, and pushed me against the bed. My tiny body bounced back and I landed on the floor.

"Get your ass up and get in the bed and stay there," she yelled.

My grandmother and Aunt Shelly witnessed the entire beating. Neither of them did anything to stop Tammie.

I jumped on the bed as fast as I could, pulled back the covers, and got underneath to hide my entire body. I cried for the rest of the night until I fell asleep.

Since I shared a room with Aunt Shelly, I witnessed first hand the agony she felt as a result of the abortion. She cried every day and every night. Now and again, she would say, "My baby. They took my baby."

In my innocence, I thought she wanted a doll like mine but they would not get one for her. I still did not understand what actually happened. I felt so badly for her and would even cry with her sometimes. Aunt Shelly treated me nicely all the time. On the inside she was really a little girl like me. Thinking she just wanted a doll to play with, I offered to let her play with Sugar. She never accepted.

It was not until later in my life that I learned Cedric got Aunt Shelly pregnant at the movies. I think looking back I don't believe that Tammie beat me because I withheld the information. And I don't think she beat me because I "let" my aunt get pregnant. I truly believe she beat me because Cedric cheated on her and never came back.

You're probably wondering why I never said anything about what I saw at the movies that night. Well, my answer is simple: it all seemed normal to me.

FOUR

The Fear; "Everyone will Hurt you, RIGHT?"

I WAS VERY CAREFUL TO CHOOSE MY WORDS WISELY WHEN telling my story to my children. Many blanket statements were used to offset the actual foul language Tammie hurled at me. The gross details of the beating and the results of the beating were minimized as well. Although I wanted my children to be aware of that aspect of my childhood, their mental and emotional well-being was a priority. They were still very young and I had to protect them.

It was quite obvious that my sharing touched them deeply yet differently. At times, Courtney would hold my hand, especially if I really began to cry. Naturally, she would cry as well. My two sons, who really did not say too much during the meeting, would often look away to keep me from seeing their tears. Of the four, Katlyn was the saddest. She cried most of all throughout and asked along the way, "Granma did that to you, Mommy? Why would she do something like that when she treats us so good?"

I decided that we all take a break. We had been sitting in the same spots for over an hour and really needed to stretch and get some fresh air. Each child picked up their practically untouched snacks and placed them back in the kitchen. Then, Courtney and Christopher went to their bedrooms and closed the door. I could hear Christopher playing his guitar and Courtney talking to one of her friends on the phone. Xavier and Katlyn ran outside to play with their friends for a while. I went to the bathroom to wash my face. Then I stepped out on the porch for a minute.

It took a minute for me to clear my mind. *I can not believe I am really sharing my life with my children. Is it still too soon? Should I end the meeting and tell them we'll get together again another time?* I was tossing around question after question in my mind. The details were about to get more explicit. I decided to call my neighbor and asked if Xavier and Katlyn could spend a few hours with her children. As always, she welcomed them with open arms and they welcomed the time to play with their friends.

After getting Xavier and Katlyn settled, I returned home and called Courtney and Christopher back to the family room. They looked a little refreshed from the break and eagerly resumed their spots. Just as I was about to speak, Courtney asked, "Mom, are you OK? I mean, do you need to do this another time?"

I AM THE ANCESTOR

"I'm fine, Baby," I said. "I've waited too long to talk to you guys about this and, as hard as it is to talk about what I experienced, I know that the time is now. No matter what I tell you, though, I do not want you to hate your grandmother. I don't. I feel very sorry for her because somewhere in her life she did not receive the love she deserved. So the "love" she tried to give me was all she knew how to give."

Christopher looked at me in the most unconvincing way. "Mom, she could have tried a little bit harder. You know, like go to the library and get a book on 'How to Love Your Daughter' or something. What she did was wrong and she knows she was wrong. It just ain't right."

My little man of the house was being protector. I so admired his strength and compassion. "Christopher, believe it or not, there were some happy and fun times in my life, too. Unfortunately, there was not that many. But, what I want you to focus on from this point until I finish telling you the story of my life is that God loves me and you and all of us. He has blessed us all to be here and has given us a good life, a very good life. My pain has great purpose. I know that one day I'm going to tell my story to the world and it's really going to help everyone who listens."

Then, I continued.

****

A few months after Shelly was forced to have an abortion,

Tammie started dating a man named Frank. He was very nice and really loved Tammie. She obviously loved him, too, but would always tell my grandmother, "It ain't nothing serious. He just somebody to hang out with, that's all." Well, for something that wasn't serious, they sure hung out a lot.

When I was about seven years old, Tammie and Frank got married. Frank moved in with us at my grandmother's house and always made sure we knew it was only for a little while. Tammie insisted that I call him "Daddy." I didn't mind. It felt nice to be able to call someone that. I was around seven years old. Frank was nice and never beat me. In fact, it seemed that the beatings from Tammie slowed down. She really began to focus a lot of her attention on Frank and doing whatever it took to make him happy.

Tammie and Frank would hit the town every weekend. Clubs and bars were their usual spots to visit. Sometimes, it would be close to daybreak when they got back home. When they were not at the club, they were out shopping. Sometimes, they would take me out to the playground or to the movies. Other times, they would often leave me home with my grandmother and uncles. One uncle in particular, Samuel, was left in charge of me often.

One of the most heart wrenching scenes from "The Color Purple" was when Sophia, played by Oprah Winfrey, stated, "A girl child ain't safe in a house full of men." It's true. I lived with my three uncles and grandfather and safety was never the norm. I guess that's why seeing my aunt's skirt up and her panties down that day at the drive-in movie did not raise a red flag in my mind.

Uncle Samuel was very tall and mild mannered. He smoked cigarettes here and there and enjoyed drinking beer throughout the day. I don't really recall him having a job, but he was never without money. He kept a wad of bills in his front left pocket all the time. My grandmother appeared to like him the best and did whatever she could to keep him happy. Out of all of her children, Uncle Samuel was the most helpful and respectful towards her. Whenever she needed him to do something around the house, he did so with no hesitation.

Uncle Samuel was what I would call a "smooth operator." He quickly found a method to build my trust. Knowing my love for cartoons, he would tell me to come in the room with him and suggest we watch them together. He would let me watch whatever channel I wanted. Usually, he would ask to hold my hand and gently massage it while we sat together on the couch. When the commercials came on, Uncle Samuel would glance at me from the corner of his eyes and say, "Ain't that funny?" as he laughed and pointed to the television. Easily humored, I would laugh really hard and he would always say, "Bolie, your laugh is making me laugh!"

I must admit: I really liked the attention. When we did not watch television, we would play games or act like we were in the movies. Uncle Samuel seemed a far cry from Tammie. He never cursed at me and never beat me. Although the way his hands touched mine felt a bit unusual, at least he touched them. It was a far cry from them being grabbed and yanked along with my tiny body by Tammie.

I clearly remember the day our cartoon watching took a turn for the worse. Not wanting to be bothered with me, Tammie and my entire family left me home while they went to the park for a cookout. Uncle Samuel said he did not want to go because it was too hot outside for him so he gladly volunteered to keep an eye on me.

As they were preparing to leave, I begged Tammie to please let me go. I promised her that I would be good and not get into any trouble. My grandmother came to my defense and demanded that Tammie let me go to the cookout, too. She paid neither of us any attention. Instead, Tammie grabbed her bag, thanked Uncle Samuel for watching me, and walked out the door. I ran to the window and began to cry as I saw them all pile in our station wagon.

Tammie got in the driver's seat. *She is always in control of something.* Just as she was about to leave, Tammie rolled down her window and yelled, "Go sit down somewhere, Chile'!" Then, she drove off. I stayed there and watched them drive out of sight. When I couldn't see them any longer, I stopped crying and returned to the living room.

Uncle Samuel was sitting on the couch quietly watching television. When he saw me begin to move he said, "Bolie, go on and wash your face then come back in here and watch cartoons with me. I think 'The Road Runner' is about to come on. I got some chips for us, too, so hurry back, OK?"

Watching "The Road Runner" and munching on chips with Uncle Samuel certainly wasn't a cookout in the park, but it was better than nothing. I ran upstairs to the bathroom to wash my face. I looked at myself in the mirror and said out loud, "What is wrong with me? Why does she hate me so much? What did I do to make her so angry this time?" The mirror never did answer me back. I wiped away the last dried tear streak from my face and ran back downstairs with Uncle Samuel.

Waiting with a big bowl of chips in the living room, Uncle Samuel said, "Hurry up, Bolie. It's about to come on now!" I jumped beside him on the couch, reached inside the bowl for a handful of chips, and began snacking away.

We watched television for a little while that day. Uncle Samuel said he was tired of watching television and just wanted to "relax." I thought that since we were not playing a game of cards of or hide-and-go-seek that we were already relaxing. I kept watching cartoons and eating the chips.

In the most unexpected way, Uncle Samuel lifted up my skirt and began to rub my thighs. When I asked him what he was doing he said, "I'm making you feel better. Don't worry. I won't hurt you, Bolie. I promise."

He continued to rub my thighs with one hand and then grabbed my panties with the other and began to pull them down. Uncle Samuel had never done this before and I could not understand why he felt this was the best way to make me feel better.

I began to get nervous and started moving away from him. As I did, he laid me down on the couch and said, "You'll feel better, Baby. Don't you trust your Uncle?"

I trusted Uncle Samuel more than anyone in the house. After all, he never beat me, curse at me, or punish me. He would let me watch whatever I wanted to watch on the television and gave me chips and other snacks to eat. Nobody else ever did those things for me. *He won't hurt me. He promised.*

I was now laying flat on my back. Uncle Samuel lifted my skirt over my face, pulled my panties down to my ankles, and opened my legs with his hands. "Keep them like this," he said softly. I heard him unbuckling his pants and slide down his zipper quickly as the sofa shifted a bit.

"Uncle, what are you about to do?" I asked innocently.

"I already told you, Bolie. I'm going to make you feel better," he said somewhat anxiously.

He won't hurt me.
He promised.
He won't hurt me.
He promised...

I AM THE ANCESTOR

Uncle Samuel began breathing very hard. I heard him say something but could not make out his words. I then felt his hands touching my private parts. I jumped back a bit. He stopped but began to use a little force to keep my legs open and started breathing heavier. I became scared and said, "Uncle...Uncle?" but he did not respond.

Uncle Samuel climbed on top of me and started to rub his penis on the outside of my vaginal area. As he continued to do this, the rubbing became harder and harder to the point of burning. I kept my eyes closed and held very still. I felt myself about the cry, but fought hard to hold back the tears.

With a very loud grunt, Uncle Samuel ejaculated all over my stomach. Firmly he said, "Don't move!" I held perfectly still not knowing what to expect next. I was tempted to remove my skirt from my face, but I just could not bring myself to do it.

My uncle jumped up from the couch and ran upstairs. I could hear him stumble a bit as his belt hit the floor. When he came back, I felt him wiping my stomach with a wet cloth, his breathing almost back to normal. He then pulled my panties back up and lowered my skirt. Our eyes met, but then I looked the other way. I was confused...very confused about what just happened.

As my uncle began to sit me back up, he asked, "Are you OK?"

I shook my head very slowly to let him know that I was even though I really was not. I kept my eyes fixed on the door hoping that my family would return. Uncle Samuel no longer seemed safe to be around. In a way, he had become "one of them" - someone that I felt would hurt me for no reason at all.

What happened next nearly paralyzed me. Uncle Samuel grabbed my hand and began to rub it the way he always did and said, "If you say anything, you know what Tammie will do to you. And if you don't play with me, I'll tell Tammie you were being a bad girl and she'll beat you." Those words gripped and held me forever.

From that day forward, Uncle Samuel started to find more games to play, movies to act out, or cartoons to watch. From time to time, we would do all of this in his bedroom. His favorite game was "Pity-Pat" because it would lure me closer to him. Eventually, the routine of him being stimulated by rubbing his penis on the outer area of my vagina changed. There were times when I would have to touch his penis, kiss it, or perform oral sex. Sometimes he would make me do all three during the same game.

Uncle Samuel began molesting me when I was about four or five. This went on for a very, very long time and no one ever knew. Uncle Samuel would take me in closets or in other bedrooms if no one was home, but mostly he would take me in the attic. There were more than enough places for him to lure me to carry out these acts. He began coaching me on what to do and how to do it and even used his abuse to make me think he was actually protecting me from Tammy. Fearing her beatings more than his molestation, I began to purposely stay near him when Tammie was around. I hated it all but I felt so trapped. One time I thought about telling Frank, but I knew he would tell Tammie and that meant getting beat. So, I said nothing.

One day while using the bathroom, I let out a scream and quickly grabbed my mouth. My vaginal area began to burn so badly. I had to urinate in small streams to stop the stinging. When I began to wipe myself, I looked down only to realize that I was bleeding. When I finished, I ran to tell my mother.

"Mommy, something is wrong with me," I said with fear in my voice.

"What are you talking about, Girl!" she said while not even looking my way.

"I'm bleeding," I said.

Tammie turned around to see where the blood was. "I don't see no blood, Bolie," she replied as if not to believe me.

I pointed to my pubic area and said, "I'm bleeding down there."

Tammie jumped up, grabbed my arm and took me back upstairs to my bedroom. She slammed the door and told me to pull down my pants and lay on the bed. She began to open my legs and grabbed her mouth. The look on her face was one of horror. I had never seen her eyes look like that before.

She pulled my clothes back up, grabbed me again, and said, "Let's go!"

As we made our way back downstairs, my uncle asked, "What's wrong Tam?"

Tammie did not reply but looked at him in a very peculiar way. It was as if she had a feeling he was the reason behind what she saw between my legs. She grabbed her purse and the keys to the car and led me out the house. She never told anyone where she was going...including me. She looked like she had seen a ghost and was too afraid to talk.

We must have drove for about ten minutes. Tammie did not say a word the entire time. When she finally parked the car, we ended up at a doctor's office. We went inside and Tammie told me to go sit down. She signed me in at the desk, told the nurse that our visit was an emergency, and then came to sit beside me. Because we did not have an appointment, she was told that I would be seen as soon as possible.

Finally, my name was called and we made our way to a room. A nurse came and took my vitals and then told us the doctor would be with us shortly. After a few minutes longer, the doctor came to see me.

"So, Symbolie...did I say that right?" he asked.

I AM THE ANCESTOR

I shook my head "Yes."

"What brings you here today?" he asked.

Just as I was about to speak, Tammie jumped in and said, "Something's going on down there," as she pointed to my vagina.

"Well, alright," he said calmly. "Let me get a nurse in here to help us, ok Symbolie?" He then turned to Tammie and said, "In the meantime, Mom, go ahead and get her undressed from the waist down and place this cloth around her. Then help her onto the table and have her to lie down."

Tammy did as the doctor stated. Still, she said nothing to me. In fact, she barely looked my way and never touched me as a means of showing affection. She was playing with her hands very nervously and mumbling something under her breath. I was tempted to ask her what was wrong but past experiences taught me not to ask her any questions.

It was not long before the doctor came back with not just one nurse, but two. They were smiling as they walked into the room and looked to be very friendly. It made me feel a little at ease. The doctor and the two nurses went to the sink to wash their hands and put on gloves. Then they came over to me.

"Symbolie, my name is Rae. I'm the head nurse here in Dr. Jacob's office. This is Nurse Ingrid. She is here to help us today," she said.

Dr. Jacob came nearer. "Symbolie, your mother said that you are having problems in your private area, is that true?" he asked.

I looked at Tammie. She looked the other way. Then, I nodded, "Yes."

"Can you tell us what's wrong?" Rae said.

In my mind, I heard myself screaming, "UNCLE SAMUEL DID THIS TO ME!" but when I looked at Tammie for help, she glared as if to say, "You better not open your mouth!"

"Symbolie? Did you hear Nurse Rae's question? Can you tell us what's wrong" Dr. Jacobs asked.

I nodded "No."

"Well, let us take a look so we can see what's happening," Dr. Jacobs said.

Nurse Ingrid came to my side, lifted the cloth covering me, and told me to open my legs. When my legs were open, she bent down to get a closer look. When she came back up, her eyes were as wide as ever. She looked at Dr. Jacobs and stepped to the side. He then began examining me.

The pain from his touch caused me to cry. Nurse Rae came to hold my hand. Dr. Jacobs told me he was doing the best he can to be gentle, but it was not working. During the examination, Dr. Jacobs tried to take my mind off of the pain by asking me about school, what my favorite flavor ice cream was, and what I really liked to do the most. Between the pain I answered him as best as I could.

When Dr. Jacobs finished checking me, he turned to my mother and said, "She needs to be taken to the hospital right away. But, before you go, I need to talk to you in my office." Dr. Jacobs then came to my side, touched my hand and said, "You did a great job, Symbolie. Your mother is going to take you to the hospital to get some medicine that will help stop the pain and make you all better. I will come by to check on you in a few days." Then, he and Tammie left out of the room while Nurse Rae and Nurse Ingrid helped me get dressed.

****

I recall being in the hospital for a few months. I was very sick and quite weak for most of my stay. Considering what I went through at home, this was a vacation; an escape from the hell I lived every single day. The medical staff, all the Teddy bears, ice cream, and hugs…lots and lots of hugs… were unforgettable. Tammie probably came to see me about three times and one of those times she came with my grandmother and Aunt Shelly. Overall, my hospital stay was very pleasant with the exception of getting two needles in my butt every day, going bald and having to wear a wig, and never receiving a visit from Frank. It was not until I was an adult that I learned why he never came and that the reason I was in the hospital was due to contracting syphilis from Uncle Samuel.

When the day came for me to return home, I knew my fairy tale was over. No more treats for me...just pain! Seeing the house as I arrived and smelling that familiar scent of moth balls when I entered the door quickly reminded me of the daily insanity that consumed me. Uncle Samuel was still there, but stayed away from me for a while. I stayed away from him, too. However, from that point on I always lived with the thought that any minute someone was going to molest me. What child deserves that?

My life resumed as usual with chores, homework, and a few childhood activities. There were times when I would play with my cousins and other children in the neighborhood. Although they continued to make fun of me, it beat staying locked in my bedroom. Tammie was still very mean and abusive towards me. When Frank was around Tammie did not beat me as hard, but she sure did scream at me! Yelling was her primary means of communication. My grandmother tried to save me and did her best to keep me focused on school and just being a little girl. She took the time to help build my self- esteem by reminding me that it was not my fault. "Your mother is just plain ol' crazy, Chile'," she would often say.

Eventually, Tammie and Frank got their own apartment. They continued to hang out on the weekends and would even have other couples come over the house from time to time.

I AM THE ANCESTOR

Because I was too young to be left home alone, I became one of the children being dropped off at my grandmother's home. Uncle Samuel still lived there at the time. I strived to stay under my grandmother for protection but he would always find a way to lure me into a place where he could perform those sexual acts. He constantly reminded me not to tell anyone or else I was going to get beat by Tammy. So, I didn't.

At my new home with Tammie and Frank, I had my own room for the first time in my life. I was so happy! I remember the good times we had as I tried to gain a sense of what it meant to be a family. Some of my fondest memories were Tammie and Frank making their own cigarettes and lining colorful bottles called "Mickies" all in a row. During Christmas and Easter, I could always count on getting toys, candy, and a new outfit or two. It was very clear that Frank was serious about being a father to me. He began to teach me how to swim and how to defend myself with Karate. He would spend time with me and share stories about his life in the military. I enjoyed being around Frank because he made me feel very safe and secure. I can still hear him say, "Bolie, you a smart girl. Always remember that."

Being in that family environment brought a little happiness and enjoyment into my life. It also brought some relief from those terrible beatings by Tammie. Now school, the holidays, and a simple game of cards were much more fun. I even had my first birthday party experience at the age of nine! Life was great!

One Saturday morning, I got up a little later than usual. Frank had already gone to work and Tammie was still in the bed sleep. I went downstairs to get a bowl of cereal and brought it back to the bedroom. I then turned on the television to watch a few cartoons while sitting at the foot of their bed. I did not have much of an appetite, so I decided to lay down and finish watching the cartoons. As I did, I noticed the bed dressings had tassels that dangled just above the floor. I started blowing them. I liked how they danced a bit and then got right back in line with the others.

Not too far from where I sat were a pack of matches. Curiously, I lit the match, placed it next to the tassel, and instantly it disappeared. This excited me! Instinctively, I struck another match and then another watching the tassels disappear one by one. I struck another match and turned my attention back to the cartoons thinking the lit tassel would immediately disappear like all the others. Just as I was about to strike another match, I realized that the bed was on fire and that Tammie was still in the bed asleep!

I froze and could not say a word although internally I was screaming to the top of my lungs. *Mommy, Mommy…get up!* The bed became more and more engulfed in flames. Paralyzed, I knew that if she woke up that would be the end of me! I uttered a very faint sound and Tammie sat straight up in the bed. For about three seconds our eyes met. It felt like I had turned to stone. Once I saw her look at me, I went into a deranged mode and began acting wildly and screaming,

I AM THE ANCESTOR

"Mommy! Mommy!" I even tried to douse the flames with my bowl of cereal. My performance was very fake, but I did it for my survival. Tammie jumped out of the bed, grabbed me out of the bedroom, and called 911 from the kitchen. Then, we went outside and across the street.

Both the fire department and the paramedics arrived moments later. Everyone from the neighborhood started coming over to us ask us questions. The paramedics started talking to me while the fire fighters questioned others. I told them that I kept calling Tammie but she could not hear me. Considering my screams were more internal than external, that would explain why she did not respond.

The fire fighters finally finished putting out the fire and then began to walk through the house. Tammie began to hug me as we stood on the other side of the street. She had never put her arms around me before. I knew in my gut that I was in for a terrible beating. I managed to hug her back and go along with the charade.

Once the fire departments investigation was complete, they walked over to where me and Tammie were.

"Ma'am, it looks like the fire initiated on your husband's side of the bed. It's possible that he had a cigarette before he went to work and did not put it out completely. That's how the bed caught on fire. I will write up the report and a copy will be on file for you at the station. You can stop by anytime after Monday afternoon to get one. In the meantime, you can go back into the house, but not into the bedroom just yet. Your bed was totally destroyed and the floor is a bit damaged. Other than that, the house is fine. Do you have any questions for me," he said.

"No," Tammy replied.

"OK. Again, my name is Sergeant Billows. Here is my number if you can think of anything else. Have a good day," he said. Then, he walked to his truck and they all left.

Tammie and I stood outside for a little while longer. Once the fire trucks were out of sight, she let me go and pushed me away from her a bit. I walked a few doors down from where she was and sat on a neighbor's porch. I began to replay what just happened and how quickly the bed caught on fire. I was glad that Tammie did not get hurt because I never wanted her to catch on fire. All I wanted was for the beatings to stop, but that had nothing at all to do with the bed catching on fire. *I will never play with matches again!*

After we stood out there for about 30 minutes more, Tammie called me and said, "Come on. Let's go back in the house."

Reluctantly, I said, "OK."

Once inside, I went straight to the kitchen and resorted to my usual routine of being busy. Tammie did not say a single word. Then out of no where, I felt both her hand around my neck and she began lifting me up off the floor.

I AM THE ANCESTOR

"I don't give a damn about what the fire department said. I know that you did it," she said through her teeth.

I started getting real dizzy from her choke hold. Then, she let me go and I landed on the floor. The one time she did not beat me was the one time I deserved to be beat. That fire was really my fault.

From that day forward, Tammie never spoke about the incident again and it did not come up in Frank's presence either. She would glare at me rather strangely from time to time. I always wondered what she thought. I'm sure in the back of her mind she always wondered if that was my plan. I bet she may have even warned herself to be careful. I mean, really, she slept in the bed that I accidentally set on fire. Surely, she must have been concerned for her own safety.

Assumed Age - 3

This is the earliest picture that I have in my possession to attempt verification of my age, and the beginning of my unhappiness, if it weren't for this picture I wouldn't have any memories of my early childhood years at all.

Assumed Age - 6

This picture displays my indifference to the Christmas Holiday. I was actually glad that it was over. "Symbolie, go up in the attic and find my coat." This was the day that I discovered four toys in a box near her coat. Assuming the age that I was I peeked at the toys and turned to meet her eyes. Know after the beating I received, the toys were trashed... I hated that silver tinseled Christmas tree anyway!

Assumed Age - 7

Although I appear to be happy, I am very tensed; I had to be careful not to mess up my good dress, scuff my shoes and keep every hair in place. I was expected to return home from school the way I left that morning..... or else.

Assumed Age - 8

Here, I am seated on the infamous "Burning Bed." Eating breakfast, lunch and dinner was a daily ritual in their room - my step-father to the left of me, while she was to my right. (Why, I am eating on a chair at the foot of a bed when there's a perfectly good dining room table in the other room....hmmm? Inquiring minds want to know.)

FIVE

Time Never Flies By; There was Never Any Fun

GETTING A SENSE OF WHAT COURTNEY AND CHRIS-topher felt was somewhat challenging. They had the blankest stares on their faces and did not say a word. I felt a strong need to stop, but I just couldn't. That probably would have done more harm than good. I had shared too much up to this point. I couldn't just leave them hanging like that. *I must tell them my story before I die.*

"Christopher? Courtney? Are you both OK?" I asked.

Christopher dropped his head between his knees. I could hear that he was starting to cry which is something he does only when necessary. I am teaching my sons that crying does not take anything away from their manhood. In fact, it really makes them stronger. Anyone who is able to express himself through tears is really a pillar of strength.

The mother in me wanted to drop everything and just go

hold him. Since we are all very emotional people, I pictured us getting stuck right there. In spite of that, it was important for me to let Christopher know that I was there for him and that I sensed his pain. Very subtly, I slid over to where he sat and just placed my hand on his back. The moment I touched him, he sulked a bit and cried even more. I did not say anything. I just allowed him to work through his emotions.

Courtney looked out of the window for a moment. Then, she turned and looked at me without saying a word. I knew that look well. It was the look of wanting to hurt someone for hurting her mother so badly. It was the look of pity. It was even the look of remorse as if she was sorry for all the times she may have not done her chores on time or forgot something at school she needed to help her complete her homework.

"If you want me to stop, I will," I said. I will understand if you don't want to hear anymore. I know it's hard on you. Children? Children?"

"Don't stop, Mommy," Courtney said softly. "We just need a little time to take it all in, that's all."

"Christopher?" I said.

Christopher lifted his head, looked at me, and shook his head from side to side.

"Children, I really went through a lot growing up and I know it's not easy for you to hear it all. This is why I'm so determined to protect you at all cost. I will never let anyone do to you what has been done to me. Never! I know that I would kill somebody if they ever laid a wrong hand on you. Period," I said, firmly.

"We know, Mommy," Christopher said. "But, because we know you to be the way that we've always known you to be....but are hearing the other way that you had to live...huh" he said, pausing to collect himself. "Well, Mommy, it's just hard to believe that Gran...Grandma would do that to you," he continued.

"Christopher, Mommy understands. Believe me I do, Son. But I want you to think about it this way: I'm still here! I'm still alive! I have four beautiful children who will never experience what I experience because I will never treat you the way I was treated. My terrible childhood was very painful, of course. But, I made it. I survived!" I said, proudly.

"Now, what I'm about to share with you next are just a few more stories of my childhood experiences. Children, my childhood was not like yours at all. It was not one filled with love; it was not filled with the type of love that I show you. This is not going to be easy to share but I know that in the end we will all be alright. If at any time it becomes too much for you to handle, please tell Mommy right away and I will stop sharing, OK??" I said.

Not wanting to miss a beat, I quickly resumed and continued to the very end.

****

The fear of Tammie's horrific beatings continued to reign in my life. No matter the time of day, a beating was just waiting for me. Believe it or not, I never wanted to retaliate. The desire to "get even" with Tammie did not enter my mind. When my younger cousins would talk to me in private, they would encourage me to plot something terrible against her. I was crippled by fear and just could not bring myself to be revengeful.

It took nothing to set her off. Her temper was out of control and the slightest thing I did that made it look like I was against her was reason for her to beat me. One such incident was when Tammie came to me for my opinion about something she had chosen to wear. She was planning to go to the bar with some friends and I was watching television when she smiled and asked me, "How do I look?"

Tammie was standing there in a nice leather pants suit with matching shoes. Her hair was done very neatly and she even had on makeup. She actually looked very pretty. However, as I was about to answer her, I said, "Ummmmm..." Tammie's smile dropped and that familiar scowl reappeared on her face.

"What the fuck you mean, 'Ummmmm...'? Ummmmm,

what, Bolie? You trying to say I'm ugly and shit or something like that? Who the fuck are you to call somebody ugly? You the ugly one, not me," she screamed.

Tammie then grabbed her belt and began to beat me. This one did not last long, but the pain was just as severe.

"I ain't going nowhere now, Girl. You done fucked up my entire evening. Shit!" she yelled. Then she went upstairs to her bedroom and slammed the door. She ended up staying home that evening. I, too, went to my bedroom. I got in the bed and went to sleep.

****

Growing up as a latchkey kid meant I was usually home alone after school. Because Tammie was so controlling, she did not allow me to be unsupervised for long. My routine was fairly simple: get a snack, do my chores, and then do my homework. Tammie made it perfectly clear that I was not to have any of my friends come over to play and that I was to not let any adults in the house while she was not there. She would always say, "You don't want anybody to grab you and take you away from me, do you?" *Yes, I do. Maybe then I won't get beat.*

One day in particular, Tammie informed me that a close friend of hers would be stopping by the house around the same time I got in from school. She told me to let him in to pick up "something" she left for him in the kitchen. When he left, I was to lock the door behind him. It sounded like a simple task and one that would not land me in a heap of trouble. Boy was I wrong!

While doing my homework, the doorbell rang. It was Mr. Trent from down the block. He told me that he had come to get a package Tammie left for him. Naturally, I let him in and pointed him to the kitchen. I returned to the dining room and continued to do my homework. Not even five minutes later, Mr. Trent was making his way to the front door, told me he got was he came to get, and left. I locked the door behind him and returned, once again, to the living room.

Tammie arrived home a little later than usual, close to 6:15 p.m. Apparently she missed the bus and had to wait an entire 30 minutes for the next one to arrive. She was tired and looked like she did not want to be bothered by anyone. I knew to stay out of her way, so I said, "Hi, Mommy," and went straight to my bedroom. I didn't event wait for her to speak back. Most of the time, she didn't anyway. Frank was still at work. He normally came home after seven in the evening.

I continued with my routine and began getting my clothes ready for the next day. I ironed them and hung them on the closet door. Then, I went to the bathroom to run the water in the tub to take a bath. All of a sudden, I heard Tammie screaming my name to the top of her lungs. I turned off the water and went to see what she wanted.

"Bolie? Did Mr. Trent come over?" she yelled.

"Yes, he did," I replied innocently.

"Well, what the hell happened?" she continued.

I said, timidly, "Nothing, Mommy! You said to let him in so I did."

"Well," she screamed, "who told you to give him any food? Why did you let him come in and eat the food out of the refrigerator, Bolie?"

At this point, I'm terrified. "Mommy, I didn't give him any food. He went in the kitchen to get what you told him to get and then he left. I didn't give him any food, Mommy. I promise I didn't!" I tried to explain.

Unbeknownst to me, Mr. Trent had gone into the refrigerator and eaten the food Tammie planned to prepare that evening for dinner. Tammie was livid and came storming right at me. Naturally, I became the target of blame for Mr. Trent stealing our dinner. Tammie gave me specific instructions and I followed them. How was I to know that Mr. Trent was going to get what he came for and take our food in the process?

This beating was like all the other: severe. I tried to move away from her, but she would grab my legs and pull me back. Tammie wailed on my body over and over until she got tired. When she finished, I literally had to crawl back to the bathroom. To have walked away from that one would have been a miracle.

****

Uncle Horace was left to care for all the children on Saturday afternoon while Tammie and my grandmother went grocery shopping. He had a thing for racetracks. It was never uncommon for him to pile us all in his car and take us to a professional racetrack. This particular day he borrowed Tammie's Corvette. I was around 12 years old and the oldest of all the children in his care at that time.

It took us a good twenty minutes to get to the track. Once there, Uncle Horace let us loose. We are all having a good time! The girls were running up and down the bleachers and the boys were playing near the men working on the cars. Moments like this with Uncle Horace really made me feel like a normal kid. Even though my cousins would tease me from time to time about getting beat by Tammie, I did not let that stop me from having fun. Considering it did not happen often, I made the best out of the times it did happen.

From the distance, I could see one of my cousins running towards us. He was holding something shiny in his hand screaming, "I won! I won!" As he got closer, I realized that he had a trophy.

I asked, "Did Uncle win a trophy?"

He said, "No. I won this trophy."

"You can't win a trophy. You can't even drive!" I said coincidently.

He smiled and replied, "I did win it, Bolie, because Uncle let me drive."

Uncle Horace came running over to the stands where the rest of the children were.

"Uncle," I said, "Who won this trophy?"

"Hot Rod won this trophy," he shouted as he gave him a pat on the back.

All of the children screamed and jumped around. My cousin was dancing and singing, "I won! I won! Uh huh, uh huh, I won!"

After the event, Uncle Horace took us all back to my grandmother's house. It was almost getting dark so Tammie and I went home.

Two weeks later while in the dining room doing my homework, Tammie came home from work. I greeted her cheerfully as usual. Her response was a way for me to detect whether she was in a good mood or bad mood, but on this day I really couldn't gauge it. My mother went straight to her room without saying a word. Instead, she went to the back room where Frank was watching television, gave him a kiss, and went upstairs. I knew something was about to happen. I stayed at the table and continued my home-work.

When Tammie returned she said, "So. I hear that Hot Rod won a trophy."

"Yes!" I said excitedly. "The trophy was so nice," I continued.

"When were you going to tell me that he drove my car?" she screamed.

Tammie had gotten extremely close to me. With nearly every word thereafter, she hit me with the belt.

"How…*whap*…dare…*whap*…you…*whap*…not…*whap*… tell…*whap*…me…*whap*…that he used my car?" she yelled as she hit me.

"Mommy, Mommy!" I screamed to the top of my lungs.

Continuing to scream, she said, "You are letting people walk all over us! Do you like doing that or something? Huh?"

I had been beaten many times, but this was a beating like no other. I remember getting up from the dining room table and careen into a wall until falling on the floor near the front door. I was dizzy as ever. I think at that moment she envi-sioned me making my escape and put all of her strength into making sure I didn't make it out. Tammie grabbed me tightly and pulled me back towards her.

Just as Tammie was about to land another whap, Frank came out no where. He got to Tammie quickly, lifted her straight into the air, looked her in the face, and said, "No more! You hear me, Tam? No more! Don't you put your hands on that girl no more!"

I had never seen Frank handle her like that. My angels were truly watching over me that day.

****

It seemed my life was out of control. After that beating, my grades began to suffer. Tammie finding out about my grades meant another beating. I had to keep this from her to save my life. So when my teacher requested that Tammie sign my failing assignments, I forged her signature.

The teacher, who obviously detected that it was not Tammie's signature, called the house. Frank answered the phone. Even though I knew I was going to get in trouble, I felt it was a blessing that he got the call first.

"Bolie, what's going on?" he asked.

"I don't know, Daddy," I said sadly.

My hope was that he would have handled it on his own. Instead, I found myself standing in the bedroom between them.

"Oh, so you want to be me, huh? You want to sign my name right?" she asked sarcastically, swinging a belt in her hand.

I AM THE ANCESTOR

Just as I braced myself to get hit, she handed Frank the belt and said, "You do it! You're always saying I'm too hard on her, so you go beat her."

I was shocked and relieved at the same time. I began to cry as Frank took me by the hand and led me to my bedroom. He closed the door and began to yell at me.

"You signed your mother's name? This is ridiculous, Girl! You know better," he screamed.

I flinched in anticipation of the belt getting ready to meet my skin as it had done so many times before. What happened next changed my outlook on Frank forever. As he continued to yell, he raised his hand and then slammed the belt down on the bed continually. Although I was still crying, he looked at me as if to cue me to scream. It did not take me long to realize that Frank was helping me. In fact, he actually saved my life!Satisfied with him handling me, Tammie went about cooking dinner. Frank let me come back down stairs and demanded that I sit next to him and watch the news. The remainder of the evening went by without further incident. I was relieved but still shaken. I just could not help wondering when my next beating would come.

****

Uncle Samuel was finally preparing to move into his own apartment. While out shopping with Tammie, we decided to stop by to check out his new place, but no one was home.

Tammie decided to go around the back of the place and have a look inside.

"Looks nice," she said, dryly. Then she looked at me.

"Oh," I said.

Not wanting to hang around too long, we got back in the car and headed home.

A few days later while I was at my grandmother's house, my grandfather referenced Uncle Samuel's upcoming move. Seeing no harm in chiming in, I shared that I saw the apartment and that I thought it was nice. I went on to say that Tammie looked in the window and that she thought it was nice also. My grandparents didn't say anything further. Instead, they looked at me rather strangely and then looked away.

A few days, Tammie called me into her room. Sitting on her bed smoking a cigarette, she looked out the window and said, "You just don't get it do you? I mean, you either want to get it or you don't want to get it! You run your fucking mouth too much but don't know who to run your mouth to! I'm grown!"

It dawned on me at that moment that my grandparents mentioned to her the conversation I had with them. It was innocent enough and true, so why was I in trouble? Without warning, Tammie grabbed a two by four piece of plywood and began to pound me endlessly. She hit me on my right side, in my stomach, and on every part of my back she could find. I tried to run to the other side of the room, but she had already backed me into a corner and I was slowly making my way down to the floor. *Help me, God! Help me...please.*

After the tenth or eleventh hit, the doorbell rang. Breathing hard from her "workout", Tammie laid the plywood against the wall, told me to get up from the floor, wiped my face as hard as she could, and sat me down on the bed. She then left the bedroom to open the door and saw that it was her best friend June.

"Hey, June!" I could hear her say.

"What's up, Tammie?" June replied.

They stayed downstairs for a while then came back to the bedroom. I did my best to appear normal; I struggled to smile. I waved at June. She waved back, exchanged a few pleasantries with me, and gave me a hug. The mere touch of her hands on my back caused me to jump a bit. The pain was bad. She didn't seem to notice because she just kept smiling and making small talk with me.

After a moment Tammie left the room to use the bathroom. Then something unusual happened: I got up enough courage to say something to June about what Tammie did. I thought that if ever I was going to be saved from Tammie and her horrible beatings, now was the time. Since the bathroom was not too far from the bedroom, I knew I had to be very quiet...and quick.

I did my best to catch June's eye. When I noticed she was looking, I reached over and began to pat the plywood trying desperately to send her a non-verbal signal. Then, I lifted my shirt and showed her my red, swollen right side.

June noticed what I did and began to make sense of what I did not say. Her eyes widened and began to water. She covered her mouth, let out a slight gasp and whispered, "Did she beat you with that?" *YESSSSSSSS! Help me, Miss June. Help me...please.*

My lips parted but I couldn't speak. The tears immediately began to pour out of my eyes. I couldn't keep them from flowing. Just then, Tammie was heading towards the bedroom. I turned away to keep Tammie from seeing me cry. I would have gotten more of the same had she thought for one minute I said something.

"Tammie, I gotta go, Girl. I just stopped by to see you for a minute. I'll give you a call later," June said. Then, she left. After that day it was a very long while before June came back. When she finally did, it wasn't to save me and nothing more was mentioned about what she saw.

****

Over the years, there were many people Tammie knew

that entered in and out of our lives with no intervention. There were signs of me being abused, some more obvious than others, yet help never came my way. June came close, but did not follow through. How could someone look at a purple bruise on a child's face, accept that "she fell down while playing", and not once question how, when, where, and why? How could that same someone, who actually witnessed Tammie go into a rage for no reason at all, not stop her when that rage was clearly directed towards me?

One summer a woman named Eleanor Thomas came from Delaware to visit Tammie. She had three children named Stevie, Daryl, and Rachel who came with her. They were about seven, eight, and nine years old. Eleanor drove to Baltimore to drop them off with Tammie who agreed to keep them for the weekend while she went to Virginia to visit a friend. Before she left, Eleanor told her children she would "really" be back as they cried and begged her not to leave them. Tammie turned to Eleanor and said, "You better!"

Eleanor had a habit of dropping her children off and disappearing for days, weeks, and even months. Even though she heard of how Eleanor would be "missing in action" for long periods of time, Tammie made sure she told her what she would do if she left her children there. Convinced that Eleanor understood, Tammie agreed to keep all three of her children. Boy was she fooled. The weekend came and went and before Tammie knew it Stevie, Daryl, and Rachel were there for the entire summer. With no sign of Eleanor in August, their summer visit rolled right into the school year. I guess that was the reason for the children's tears and Tammie's comment, neither of which kept Eleanor true to her words

I remember Tammie saying something like, "I can't believe that bitch stuck me like this. Somebody's going to pay for this shit." I knew one way or the other that 'somebody' was going to be me. Unfortunately, those three children who were left against their will had to pay, too. The four of us were blamed for everything from the door being left opened to eating the last piece of bread. Never mind that other family members were in and out of the house all day. The finger was always pointed at us and we all got beat.

Tammie pretty much left us to fend for ourselves when it came to breakfast. It was bad enough that she had to cook breakfast for one child. Cooking breakfast for the four of us was, of course, out of the question. Usually we would just make a bowl of cereal, but decided to only get toast one morning. There was barely enough butter for our bread, but we managed to get enough of what was left on each piece of toast to make it enjoyable.

Later that morning, Tammie went into the kitchen to make her a few slices of toast and realized there wasn't any butter left.

"Who the fuck used up all the butter?" she screamed from the kitchen.

"Mommy, it was only a little bit left," I explained. "We put the rest on our toast for breakfast," I continued.

"OK," she said in a threatening way.

We were terrified! We expected Tammie to come storming out of the kitchen and beat us all. However, she just went back upstairs to her room and slammed the door. We were all relieved, but I felt in my stomach that she was going to get us one way or the other.

The next day, Tammie woke up earlier than usual. By the time we made it to the kitchen, she had already toasted a few slices of bread for us. It even had butter on it. She must have gone to the store early that morning.

"Sit down and eat," she said. Then she slid a plate to each of us with two slices a piece.

After we each ate a third slice and were about to leave the table, she told us to sit back down. Tammie then went to the toaster, and toasted four more slices of bread and made us eat it. Again, we tried to get up after we ate the fourth slice, but she would not let us. Tammie continued to make more and more toast and forced us to eat each slice she ate."You think you can eat all of my butter and get away with it? Do you?" she screamed.

Each of us sat there crying as we ate the dry pieces of toast. Then, Rachel began to vomit.

"What the fuck..." Tammie screamed. "You better hold

that shit in, damn it," she said louder than she screamed.

Rachel was horrified! She tried to keep from vomiting but then began to choke and let it all out right on the table.

Tammie ran over to her, slung the chair away from the table, and pushed Rachel on the floor. Rachel crawled to the corner by the refrigerator, and sat there and cried. The rest of us stayed at the table and cried because we were too afraid to move.

"Get the hell out of my kitchen," Tammie said to us all. As quickly as we could, all of us ran upstairs to my room and stayed there for the rest of the day. Stevie, Daryl, and Rachel stayed close to each other from that point forward and cried for their mother everyday.

About two weeks later, their mother called. Tammie cursed at Eleanor terribly and then said, "Well why didn't you tell me? Sure, they can stay until next week." I'm not quite sure what happened kept Eleanor away in Virginia for so long, but it was obvious that Tammie understood.

Tammie then gave the phone to Stevie. He was crying and telling his mother they wanted to go back home. He told her what Tammie did with the toast and how Rachel threw up. Then, he gave the phone to Daryl and Rachel who were begging for her to pick them up. They listened to their mother and then said, "Yes, Mommy. We promise." Then, they hung up the phone. Daryl turned to Stevie and said, "Mommy wants us to make sure we are good because it can't be that bad here." Well, she was wrong. It was worse than bad.

All four of us children got along good. After the toast experience, we sort of developed a bond that helped us look out for each other. Aside from the need to survive while living with Tammie, we were typical children who liked to play and watch TV. We had gotten close in the short period of time they were there. I really did not want them to leave.

One day, that bond was challenged in a way I had never imagined. Living with Tammie left me with many terrible memories, but the memory of what I'm about to tell you stuck in a way I never thought it would. Rachel, the youngest of us all, once forgot to make my bed that we shared. Tammie was livid!

"Bolie, you and those other kids better get your asses in here," she demanded.

We all ran upstairs as scared as ever.

"Which one of you didn't make this bed this morning?" she asked.

Even though we all knew it was Rachel, we did not respond.

"Somebody better fucking answer me and now," she screamed.Rachel raised her hand and then started to cry.

"Shut up, damn it. Don't start that crying shit now, Girl. Don't you know you suppose to make this damn bed when you get up, huh?" she asked.

Rachel just shook her head. Then, Tammie turned to me and said, "Take her little ass outside and wear it out, Bolie. If I hit her, I'll go to jail. That little redbone will look like a bunch of strawberries," she said.

I did not know what to do, so I stood there for minute.

"Did you hear what I said? You better grab her ass and beat the hell out of her or I'll do to you what I want to do to her," she informed me.

So, I grabbed Rachel by her little arm, took her downstairs, and out the door. Tammie was right there to make sure I did what she made me do.

"That's right! Drag her little ass out the door," Tammie instigated.

Stevie and Daryl were calling out loud for their mother and Rachel and I were crying. Tammie was telling all of us to shut up. I felt terrible beating Rachel for no reason at all. A few times, I purposely swung at the air to miss hitting her. I really didn't want to hit her at all, but to not do it meant I would get a beating worse than the one I was giving her. I was so sad because Rachel and her brothers had become like family to me in the short time they were there with us. They were really very nice children who did not deserve to be abandoned by their mother and left with someone like Tammie.

I AM THE ANCESTOR

A few days later, Eleanor came back to get her three children. When she walked in the door, they jumped off of the sofa and ran straight to their mother. They started to cry a little, but Eleanor never asked why. She just said, "I'm not going to leave you anyplace else." She told them that she could not help leaving them with Tammie and promised that they would go back home and return to school.

Tammie acted like they were the best children ever who never caused her trouble. According to her, they were better children than I would ever be. Tammie even bragged on how well they helped with chores and listened to what she said. After telling Eleanor how she felt about being "left to take care of those children with no help," she told Eleanor if she needed her again to just give a little notice. What a liar!

 I would be well into adulthood before learning that Stevie and Daryl slept in the walk in linen closet where the vacuum and cleaning supplies were stored. Tammie was cruel, but I never thought she would do that to someone else's children. Our two bedroom place was small, but those boys could have slept on the couch or been given blankets to make a palette on the floor in the living room or my bedroom.

When Stevie, Daryl, and Rachel left, I was getting beat as if it were still the four of us. I kept telling myself that they would tell their mother what Tammie did to all of us. I painted a picture in my mind of all of them would call the police, tell them everything we went through those three weeks we were together, and they would all come back and rescue me. Then, Eleanor would become my new mommy and we would be together forever.

Until this very day, I have not seen Eleanor, Stevie, Daryl, or Rachel ever again.

****

After several weeks, the apartment was done and Uncle Samuel had moved. He had a girlfriend, who he beat all the time, and even a new baby. On several occasions, I was sent there for reasons unknown to this day. I guess it was to babysit, but one or both of them was typically there when I went to visit. Tammie very well could have sent me just to get a break or for no reason at all.

On one such occasion, Tammy and Frank were hanging out with a few of their friends dropped me off at his apartment. I was really hoping his girlfriend was going to be there with us, but she had taken the baby to visit her mother. I asked Tammy if I could go to my grandmother's, but she told me I couldn't. I did not want to go to Uncle Samuel's house. I had a bad feeling that going there was not going to be good for me and I was right. It was on this visit that the sexual molestation escalated to the loss of my virginity. I was only 13 years old.

After Tammy and Frank left, Uncle Samuel came and sat beside me on the couch. I could feel him looking at me, but I just kept staring at the television. He got up, turned it off, and stood me up in front of him. "You're bigger now so I gotta do more than just kiss and rub it. I been waiting on this day for so long," he said, disgustingly.

"Uncle, I don't wanna," I pleaded. "I just wanna watch television, that's all."

He did not listen. Instead, he took me down the hall and to his bedroom. He wasted no time taking off my clothes. That same heavy breathing I had heard before sounded scarier. He pushed me on the bed, forced my legs open, covered my mouth with his hand, and then penetrated me.

I just wanted to die. I felt pain before but never like that. I cried the entire time, but it was as if he didn't even hear me. I was there for a long time that day, so he repeated the act again. This time he took much longer to finish.

When Tammie and Frank came to get me, I ran to get in the car. Every step I took hurt like hell, but I just had to get out of there. When I looked back, I saw Uncle Samuel standing in the door, waving.

"I'll see you next time, Bolie," he said very cynically. Then, he shut the door.

****

When I was around 15 years old, I approached Miss June and asked her about people touching other people's private parts. She did not have any insight into my abuse; however, she was really curious to know why I was asking.

"What's this all about, Symbolie?" she said rather suspiciously. "Who's doing this to you? Is it your mom…your dad?"

I did not answer her.

"That's not right, Love. That's just not right," she said with her arms folded. Then she gave me the following advice. "If it happens, ask them to stop and then ask them why they are doing this to you."

A few months had passed and the sexual assaults by Uncle Samuel continued. They got more and more rough and even unbearable at times. I was really afraid to stand up for myself so I didn't put Miss June's advice into practice right away. However, it was not long before I built up my confidence.

During one such assault, I said to Uncle Samuel, "You have to stop! It's not right." I remembered what Miss June said and then asked him, "Why do you do this to me anyway?"

Coldly and without remorse, he replied, "Because I can! You ain't my fucking niece, anyway!" he said as he continued.

His words gripped me, but I did not say anything else. I figured he was just being his usual mean self and trying to dodge responsibility. So, I just stayed there and waited for him to finish. Years later, as I began putting the many pieces of the puzzle of my life together, that statement made more sense.

Confronting him appeared to have an effect because the sexual assaults stopped. However, he continued to grope and touch me inappropriately as often as he could

****

My menstrual cycle started around the age of 15 or 16. Instinctively I knew I could not tell Tammie. In fact, I did not tell anyone. That's a rather sad commentary but very true. While other daughters probably ran to their mother to get help and advice, I ran to the bag of clothes destined for the Goodwill and grabbed various pieces of clothes and made my own sanitary napkins. Unfortunately, this was not an effective solution but the only one I had. I never told Tammie that my menstrual cycle began and she never asked.

I never shall forget when Tammie and Frank decided to go away to Atlantic City for the entire weekend. They took me to my grandmother's, but it wasn't like old times when all of my cousins were around. We had all gotten older and were pretty much able to take care of ourselves. Tammie rarely let me stay home alone when she was going to be gone for an extended period of time.

To my surprise, my Uncle Roger, who was recently released from jail, returned home. My grandmother, grandfather, and Aunt Shelly were there, too. I had seen him a few times since his release, but nothing more than a "Hello" was exchanged. Whenever I visited, he would normally just sit in the living room and watch television. For a very long time,

I thought something was wrong with him, but never asked anyone.

The old saying, "Expect the unexpected," met me head on during one of my stays at my grandmother's. My grandparents were in the kitchen playing a game of cards and Aunt Shelly was in her bedroom. My Uncle Roger was in his usual spot on the living room couch and I was on the floor. Without warning, he grabbed hold of me and quickly took me downstairs to the basement. All of the lights were out but it was not totally dark. I remember it being very cold. I was terrified and didn't know what to do. Fear prevented me from saying a word.

He took me to the utility closet and then began to undress me. *Not another one, God. Please...help me!* Remembering what Miss June said, I tried to talk my way out of it.

I said, "We shouldn't be down here, Uncle. I want to go back upstairs."

Nothing deterred him. When I moved one way, he blocked me. When I moved the other way, he blocked me again. Finally, I sensed there was no way out and stopped resisting. He turned me around and made me bend over and then continually forced himself inside of me until he satisfied himself.

"Please don't do this to me because Uncle does it, too," I pleaded.

I AM THE ANCESTOR

My feeble attempt to let yet another person know what I was going through was met with no reply. Uncle Roger ignored me. His assault and violation continued. Unfortunately, this was not a one time act. Since he was living at home with my grandparents with no job, he made frequent appearances to my home when my parents were not there. He took advantage of the opportunity and helped himself to me.

Tammie managed a small janitorial business which provided services for various office buildings in downtown Baltimore. She hired my uncle along with eight other crew members. Because I was 16, she was able to hire me as well. I worked hard to not only keep those buildings clean but also to please Tammie. I wanted to make sure that I did not do anything to make her upset. However, the slightest mistake resulted in me getting beat. No place was off limits when it came to her abuse. Not even those office buildings.

One particular shift, I accidentally forgot to place the broom back on the cart before returning it to the closet. The beating from that simple mistake left me with a swollen arm, but Tammie did not care. I still had work to do and she expected it to be done. She screamed at me for moving slow, but what was I supposed to do? My arm was puffy as ever and the slightest move of it caused so much pain.

An hour after the beating, I found myself looking at the big glass doors of the office building. They led straight to the main street. Unconsciously, I was edging closer and closer to door. *I've got to get out of here. I can't take another beating.* My trance was broken when I heard Uncle Roger say, "Where are you going? We are not leaving. Plus, we have to leave out the back."

I truly believe he read my thoughts. He tried to comfort me.

"Your mother didn't mean to hit you, she's just frustrated," he said, unconvincingly.

Unbeknownst to me, he later shared with Tammie that he saw me about to leave through the glass doors. His revelation gave Tammie permission to scream at me in front of the crew.

"Where do you think you are going, Girl? You think you are going to run away from me?" she demanded.

"No, Mommy," I said. "I was just looking out of the doors at the cars going by, that's all. I wasn't trying to run away from you, Mommy. I promise! I wasn't trying to run away…just looking at the cars, Mommy," I lied to save myself from getting a beating.

"Don't you dare lie to me, Bolie. Where the fuck you trying to go, Girl? Where? Who in the world would want you? Nobody, that's who, because you ain't worth shit. Every time you turn around you crying over some dumb shit, you fucking up in school, and you barely work. Don't nobody want your good for nothing silly ass," she screamed.

I AM THE ANCESTOR

Tammie yelled to the top of her lungs. Her bark was just as bad as her bite sometimes. The words she used against me cut like a knife straight to my soul. That, along with the look on her face, was horrifying! It would have been fine with me for her to just yell, but I a beating was coming. Right away, Tammie started to wail on me. Whatever was within her reach became her weapon: cleaning products, cords, dust pans, scouring pads. I tried to dodge what I could, but the cluttered closet was just too small. Every corner had a shelf and every shelf held products. There was no way to escape her wrath. I just had to deal with it.

I tried really hard not focus on what she was doing. Each hit caused my body to jerk. I was in lots of pain. I began to remember how close I was to those doors. How close I was to freedom. The life I always wanted was waiting for me on the other side. No more beatings. No more verbal abuse. No more fear of the unknown. Freedom! Why didn't I just run and keep running? I was so close. So close.

When I came out of the room, the entire crew was standing there. I was covered with Ajax from my head to my feet. My eyes were burning from both my tears and the fumes from the bottle of ammonia that spilled on the floor. Tammie, too, had stains on her clothes but she did not seem to care. In fact, she walked out as if to dare anyone to question what happened. No one said a word and no one offered to help. Not one single person looked my way as I tried to make eye contact except for Uncle Roger.

Then, he simply walked down the hall and around the corner.

It would be many years later when Uncle Roger would revisit that brutal beating. He confessed how afraid he was of Tammie since they were children. Just when I thought her violence began with me, it actually began when they were teenagers. Uncle Roger told the story of how at the age of about 13 years old, Tammie and Uncle Roger got into a heated argument. Before he knew it, she had grabbed a knife and began chasing him around the house. It took both my grandparents to hold her down. Uncle Roger knew that had they not been there, he would have gotten stabbed or worse.

From that day forward, Tammie would remind him "who was boss" and that he'd better not cross the line with her. Uncle Roger never did.

A month or so later at the same job site, Tammie pulled me aside and began to explain a special assignment she had for me. I could tell by the way she called me that it had nothing to do with cleaning office buildings. In fact, her exacts words were, "I need you to help me make some extra money." Immediately, I knew what she meant. Tammie wanted me to help her with another one of her insurance scams.

Tammie was famous for running insurance scams. In the past, she had gotten large settlements from home, life, automobile, and personal property insurance companies. "Payday" is what she would call them when she shared the amount of the check that came in her name. Wherever possible, she would inure herself or have someone else do it for her. Tammie has been cut, broken bones, and nearly poisoned herself to death all for the sake of "making some extra money." As you can see, she was a sick person in more ways than one.

When Tammie approached me about her plan to have another "payday", we were providing janitorial services in a building owned by one of the largest telephone companies in the United States. They had recently moved to downtown Baltimore and we were the first cleaning company they contracted. Although I was only 16 years old at the time, Tammie always talked business in my presence. When another adult would suggest she send me to another area, she would comment, "Bolie ain't smart enough to understand what I'm talking about. She don't know nothing no way."

We had just finished our cleaning assignment for the evening. Tammie told the other workers they were free to go and that she and I would stay behind to do the final sweep to make sure we didn't miss any spots. It was Friday night and, naturally, none of the other crew members hung around. Getting of early from work meant they could get home early and get dressed to go to the club...early.

Once everyone was gone, Tammie told me she wanted to make it look as if she had fallen on a wet area or torn piece of carpet. The injury of choice this time was a broken arm, both arms if it were possible. She knew without a doubt her plan would work. The accident would be bad enough for her to sue them and rake in lots of cash. She didn't care anything about the pain she would feel from those broken arms. The thought of having all that money eased the thought of pain instantly. I can still see that sinister look on her face when her plan started to come together in her mind.

First, she needed something strong enough to break her arm. She decided to look in the supply closet first. The only thing in there that could possibly serve her purpose was a mop. But, she decided that was not going to do the trick. After pacing the floor a bit and thinking it through, she went to the basement of the building and found a steel pipe about two feet long. When she came back up stairs, she took me in the bathroom and told me in detail her plans.

"Look, I know this is your first time, but you gotta do this shit right, OK? It's gotta be done so I can go to the hospital and get a report" she said.

"Yes, Mommy," I replied.

She started walking towards the bathroom and gestured for me to follow her. Once we got inside, she went into the largest stall, got on her knees, and twisted her arm around the base if this metal and porcelain toilet.

"Come here, Bolie," she called.

Once I got inside with her, she handed me the pipe and pointed to where she wanted me to hit her on the arm.

"Look, Girl. You gotta do it hard enough for the bones to break. I mean really hard. You understand?"

I froze, slightly, but managed to slowly shake my head to let her know that I understood.

"Bolie, I swear to God, you better not fuck up and hit me anywhere else or I'll beat your narrow ass with that damn pipe, you got that?" she said while gritting her teeth. "All I need is for you to screw me over with this, damn it!" she continued.

I was petrified and could not move. As I stood there motionless, I honestly believe I stopped breathing. As much as Tammie deserved to be hit, the fear of laying a single finger on her paralyzed me. Because of all the pain, scars, bruising, and unnecessary punishment that she put on me almost daily I was well within my rights to beat her to a pulp. I could have used that steel pipe to break every bone in her body and it would have been nothing she could do. Shucks, I could have even killed her.

For as long as I can remember, Tammie has gotten paid off the sweat of my back. Although I began cleaning office buildings with Tammie when I was 16 years old, I actually began working with Tammie on odd jobs around the age of 11. Actually, I worked for her because I never, I mean never, saw any of the money except for about $20 every now and again. I did hair, laundry, clean houses, recycle cans and bottles, and more. Whatever Tammie did to make a little extra cash, she made me do...for free.

"Mommy, please..." I begged. "Please don't make me do it, Mommy. I can't!" I continued as I started crying.

Before I knew it, Tammie got up and pushed my face with the palm of her hand forcefully. My head slammed up against the wall and I went down to the floor. I cowered so not to get hit and cried even more.

As she walked away, Tammie kicked me in my leg and stepped on my arm.

"You can't do nothing right, damn it! You have fucked this up for me too, Girl. My whole life has been nothing since I got you. Wait until I get you home. You are going to wish you did what I told you to do. Get your ass up and let's go," she yelled.

I got up from the floor, looked at those glass doors, and walked out knowing that another beating was right around the corner. I also knew that because of the fear Tammie instilled in me, I would never pleaded for mercy.

SIX

A Working, High School Graduate That Still Gets Beat

THE YEAR WAS 1984 AND MY LIFE WAS LIKE SOMETHING out of the twilight zone. Everyone had moved back home to my grandmother's house including me, Tammie, and all three of my uncles. Frank was gone. He and Tammie had gotten a divorce. I am not quite sure why we had to give up the apartment. Tammie just came home from work one day and told me to pack my thing because we were moving. I did exactly as she ordered.

The living arrangements were challenging, but my grandmother made it work. My aunt and I resumed sharing a room. My grandmother and grandfather shared a room. Uncle Horace had his own room, Uncle Samuel, who was around here and there, lived in the living room or slept in the back part of the basement where the washer and dryer were, and Uncle Roger made the back of the basement his spot, and Tammie stayed in the front of the basement as if it were a private bedroom.

It was my last year in high school and the most difficult year of my life. During the day at school, all was pretty normal. I had work study and the normal load of classes for a senior. Then when I came home, I had to focus on where to hide or where to go to stay clear of my uncles. On any given day I could find myself pondering which uncle would assault me in which room of the house. I always looked for something to fix, an errand to run, or just how to stay busy and unavailable.

Uncle Samuel typically offered to drive me around when errands were on my list of things to do. Tammie thought I was stupid to reject the offer and insisted that he take me wherever I needed to go. There were times when he would drive me and seize the opportunity to assault me. It never failed and he did not care where, when, or what time of the day. He took me in an alley, a hidden grassy area, an even an old abandoned build once during the day. Whenever he wanted it, he pretty much got it.

Uncle Samuel and Uncle Roger were like a tag team. However, it appeared that they did not talk about it with each other. There acts were random and each had no clue that the other was taking advantage of me, too. Uncle Roger never flirted with me. He was very sneaky and made his move only when the opportunity presented itself. For a brief period of time, Uncle Samuel had stopped. But, once he was back in the rotation he would always allude to "catching me later."

I AM THE ANCESTOR

Tammie did hair on the side to keep extra money in her pockets. Of course, she made me do hair as well. Never did see any of the money I made. Even though I shared a room with Aunt Shelly, Tammie made it so that I would be in the basement with her daily to do hair with her. Sometimes I would be so tired from all the housework and from doing hair that I'd end up sleeping in the basement with her. Other times, I found the strength to make it back to the room with Aunt Shelly. But, Tammie would never let me stay up there for long.

I had worked close to ten hours straight one day doing hair with Tammie. I could not keep my eyes opened to save my life…so I shut them. Tammie did not like me "sleeping on the job" and she made sure I felt her displeasure.

"Bolie, go upstairs to the room and lay down," she said in a very strange way.

I was surprised she gave me a break, but glad for the chance to get rest. Before I could shut my eyes good, she came bursting through the doors.

"Get your ass up," she said under her breath.

"What's wrong, Mommy?" I asked, still woozy from being tired.

Without saying a word, Tammie grabbed me by my arm and slammed me into the wall. I bounced off and landed straight on the floor. All I felt next were her feet kicking me in my legs and on the side of hip.

"I bet you won't fall asleep on me again, will you?" she screamed.

"No," I answered.

Then, she walked out of the room and down the steps. As I struggled to get up, I noticed Uncle Roger at the door. He looked as if he had just seen a monster. Actually, he had. Her name was Tammie.

"You OK?" he asked.

I just shook my head.

Then, he looked at me and said, "I didn't know."

And from that day forward, Uncle Roger never raped or touched me again. I guess after he saw what I went through with Tammie, he did not want to cause me anymore pain.

With my graduation fast approaching, I began to really focus on leaving. *I can't continue to live like this.* I figured my way out would be through the military or nursing school. These two career paths were pushed heavily at my school. If I continued to do the right thing the right way, I thought, I could take either path and finally leave. *Do good...be good...and leave! Do good...be good...and leave! LEAVE!*

Extracurricular activities were everywhere at my school. I could not participate in many of them because proof of birth was required. Tammie never provided me a copy of my birth certificate since I began asking for it in the tenth grade. When my teachers asked why I did not sign up for an activity, I'd just tell them that Tammie could not find my birth certificate. In my senior year, I became eligible for Driver's Education. I asked Tammie for my birth certificate once more.

"Mommy, I was supposed to take Driver's Ed. Can I have my birth certificate, please?" I asked.

"You don't need to drive. And I'm not going to put you on my insurance because it will cost more," she replied.

"I don't have to drive your car, Mommy. The class is so that I can learn the manual and learn how to take the test. They will let us use their cars during the school day to practice," I said hoping she would allow me.

"Well, I'll write and apply for your card one of these days," she said.

Whenever I would follow up with her to see if she had gotten my birth certificate, I was met with one excuse after another:

"New York (the place of my birth) is a big state and it's taking so long to get your paperwork back."

"I've applied so many times. I guess I just have to go up there."

"They told me it was in the mail last week. I don't know what's going on!"

One day I told Tammie that military recruiters stopped by

the school to speak to the seniors about joining the service. I was very interested in joining the Marines. This was the best choice for me since flying airplanes or being in the water was not on my fun list. I felt really good about what they had to offer and believed Tammie would see it as a great opportunity for me. So, I applied on the spot with the recruiter who told me that my grades were good enough and everything else on the application looked good. The missing link, of course, was my birth certificate. This meant another chat with Tammie to get an update.

"Mommy, I filled out papers to join the Marines today! They have really good benefits like going to college and lifetime insurance. And I can travel for free, too," I said excitedly. "All they need is my birth certificate and that will be all. Has it come back yet?" I asked innocently.

Tammie walked right up to my face and said just above a whisper, "Who the fuck do you think you are? Those mother fuckers are just going to put you in and not talk to your family? You are not going into any fucking services! That's no career! That's just a waste of time."

"Did the birth certificate come back yet," I asked so not to forget what was really important.

"If I would have gotten it, I would have told you," she said harshly as she stepped away from me.

I simply said, "Yes, Ma'am."

I AM THE ANCESTOR

About a month later, I went to Tammie again. This time it was about a nursing program. I knew I was more than qualified to apply and figured since Tammie said no to the military then maybe she would let me do this. I found her at the kitchen table and began to share.

"Mom," I said, "there is a nursing program at the school and they said after you do their program for six months you can then go to college for two years and become a registered nurse and then we wouldn't have to pay all the money for me to go to a four year college. Plus, I got a surprise for you," I said with a big smile.

Without looking my way she said, "What surprise?"

"I saved up a deposit," I replied proudly.

If her neck were not attached to her shoulders, it would have snapped off because she whipped her head my way very hard.

"Where the hell did you get money from to save?" she snapped.

I began having second thoughts about telling her, but was too afraid to try to make up a lie. The cat was just a bit out of the bag so I had to give it total freedom.

"Well, on Fridays when I give you the check I get from helping you clean those offices and you would give me $20 back to spend, I saved it. So for a while I've been doing that and I saved $800," I said.

Tammie's eyes got very wide. I could tell that she thought I was lying.

"You couldn't have $800! Where is it? Give it to me now," she screamed.

I went to my bedroom, pulled out the box I hid way in the back of my closet underneath a pile of sweaters, grabbed the money, and ran back downstairs.

Tammie snatched it out of my hands and said, "Give me that fucking money. That's no school. What kind of fucking school lets someone go for six months? You'll probably go to jail for not knowing all that you should. I'm going to keep this since I'm saving your money for you anyway. You probably thought I spent or wasted the other money you made, didn't you?"

"No, Ma'am," I lied. I just wanted to save money for me, too," I said sadly.

"Well, I'm going to take this money to a real university that you can go to." Without saying anything else, Tammie walked out of the kitchen.

I never saw my $800 again. Not for one second did I believe Tammie was saving money for me. But, but all was not lost. I knew that I had to be a step ahead when it came to Tammie so in addition to the $800 I saved I probably had another $400 stashed away that I had stolen from my part time job as a restaurant cashier. I am not proud of doing this. It was truly all about survival. Let me explain.

The restaurant always had a weekly special that would discount the total bill by two dollars when they presented their bonus card. Back then, bonus cards were not scanned. All the customer had to do was show me to get the discount. If a customer had their bonus card, two dollars would come off of their bill, and I would note it on my tally sheet. However, on the days when they didn't have the card they paid the full price but I still noted on my tally sheet that the card was presented but I would keep the two dollars for myself. It was horrible and frightening at the same time. After weeks of doing this I managed to save the extra $400.

After that experience with Tammie, I became a little stronger somehow. Taking my hard earned money from me was just as bad as her beating me. I became more and more tired of her nasty ways. When I turned 18, I became even stronger. I began to focus more and more on getting out of that house that it consumed my every thought.

The day I had waited for all my life was finally here: graduation! It was just another day as far as my family was concerned although I was the first one in my family to graduate from high school. I thought for sure there would be some type of celebration. There was nothing. No cards, no balloons, no cake...nothing.

I waited and waited for Tammie to mention her plans to get

me in college. There were college tours taking place pretty often, but all she worried about was getting my paycheck. July went by then August. Now, all my friends are talking about going to either local, in state, or out of state colleges. By the time September rolled around and everybody I knew was attending either college or going through a program that would certify them to work a trade if they were not already working. I was getting really tired of the games Tammie was playing and decided to approach her again about my future.

"Mom, I know you are busy and working a lot, but what about me going to nursing school? I really want to do this because I kind of like it and only have to go for a few years," I said with certainty.

She replied, "No. I don't want you to go there. I want you to go to a real university."

"Well, just give me the money so I can go enroll at a real university," I said firmly.

The next thing I remember was seeing Tammie standing above me as I lay on the floor. She had both hands around my throat. I don't know how she made it from across the room so quickly and I don't know how I made it on the floor. It all happened so quickly.

"After all I've done for you? How dare you ask me for some money? Shit, if anybody need to be asking for money, it's me. After all these years I took care of you, you owe me," she yelled.

Finding strength I never knew I had, I grabbed her hands while they were still on my throat and tried to loosen the grip. I kept telling myself that I was strong enough to fight and win against her. But, no matter how much I did I just couldn't bring myself to hit her back. I just couldn't.

Thinking my attempts to loosen her hands was my way of fighting back, she yelled with surprise in her voice, "You wanna fight me, Bolie?" From there, the beating got worse. Tammie began to "defend herself" like never before as she hit and choked me with every word. I began to lose consciousness and blacked out a bit.

Faintly, I heard her say, "You will never get this money! You owe me everything you got and can never repay me, Girl." Then, she let me go, got up from off of the floor, and went upstairs.

I didn't move right away. I just laid there and thought about leaving home. After that incident, it was time *I'm 18 years old and I still get beat like a child. No more of this. I gotta get out of here!*

That next Friday when I got off from work, Tammie met me at the door. It was pay day from the restaurant so I knew what she wanted. Without saying a word, I pulled the check out of my pocket and gave it to her. I then went inside the house to change into the clothes I used to clean the office. I was so tired and did not want to go with Tammie, but that was not an option for me. When I finished changing my clothes, I went back outside and sat on the porch to wait for Tammie.

Tammie finally came out of the house and said, "We don't need you at the job tonight so you can just stay here."

It was at that moment I knew that was going to be the night for me to leave. I got energized by that thought alone, but I remained very still and continued to look tired.

As Tammie got in the van, she said, "What are you going to do tonight?"

I replied as if not to care, "Maybe I can go to the Inner Harbor or to the movies or something. I might even hang out with my friends from the restaurant."

"Look," she screamed. "Since you can't make up your damn mind, don't go no damn where! All these damn maybe's... you don't know what to do with yourself. You so stupid, Girl. Just keep your ass home and the dishes better be done when I come back, too. I thought you were 18 and graduated from high school! You don't know shit, Bolie." Then she drove off.

I stood motionless as I watched Tammie go around the corner. Here I was 18 years old and still being treated like a child. I replayed what she just said to me about being "18 and graduated from high school." Well for once, Tammie told the truth.

"You're right, Mommy," I said out loud.

I stood on the porch for a minute or so longer. When I saw that the car was out of sight, I ran back inside the house and went straight to my bedroom. I started shoving as many of my belongings in a duffle bag. When it was filled with as much of my personal belongings as I could get in there, I threw the bag out of the back window. At the time, my grandmother was the only person home with me. She was watching television in her bedroom.

"Goodbye, Grandma," I said.

"Goodbye. Where are you going?" she asked.

"Downstairs," I told her.

"OK, Bolie," she said as she continued to watch television.

I quickly went downstairs and out of the front door. I then went to the back of the house, picked up the duffle bag, and began to walk into the night. I never looked back.

SEVEN

Changing the Name Doesn't Protect the Innocent

I **WALKED TO THE BUS STOP AND GOT ON THE FIRST ONE THAT** pulled up. I took my seat and just rode around Baltimore for a while. My thoughts consumed me. I was not aware of my surroundings. My mind was racing. *Did I just run away from home?* A little more than an hour had passed and I was becoming anxious. I decided to get off the bus at the next stop…no matter where I was.

It just so happened that the next stop was right across the street from the Greyhound bus station. Just one look at those buses and I knew I was running away…from pain. It was exciting to think that I could go anywhere I wanted and never return. The only other option would be to go back home and get beat for being out of the house too long. My mind started racing again. *I don't even know where I'm going, but anywhere has got to be better than here.*

I went to a counter and grabbed the yellow pages book.

I AM THE ANCESTOR

Hesitantly, I tore out a page, spun it around, closed my eyes, and touched a spot on the page. It landed on Chicago. *It's cold there!* I went back to the yellow pages book to tear out another page. Before I opened the book, the announcer came over the P.A. system and said, "Bus number 44, gate 33 now boarding for Miami. *That's where I'm going!* I quickly ran to the ticket counter to buy my ticket.

"Name, please," the woman asked.

I was prepared to give the name that I had used all of my life: Symbolie Smith. But I thought using my real name would lead Tammie and the police right to where I was going.

"Miss, I need your name for your ticket, please," she said, interrupting my thoughts.

I replied, "Monique. Monique Smith."

As strange as this may sound, when I changed my name to Monique Smith it felt very natural. Really, a certain amount of peace came inside of me when I changed my identity. I was getting away from my family and changing my name was going to keep them from finding me. If they were going to come looking for me, naturally they would come looking for Symbolie and find me right away. But, they would have never thought to ask for me by my middle name.

In less than two hours, my entire life began to change. I no longer had a place to lay my head, I changed my name, and I was about to board a bus traveling to another part of the United States. It really felt like I was watching a play about someone else's life. But, when I heard the announcer say, "Last call for Miami," and my feet began to walk towards the gate with my ticket in hand, I knew I was the lead character.

I dashed towards the bus and boarded with everything I owned stuffed inside of my duffle bag. I was happy, excited, and a bit nervous as the bus began to pull away from the gate. Visions of Tammie rolling up in her car, finding me on the bus, and demanding the bus to stop circled in my head. I could see her jumping on board, grabbing me, and dragging me back to the car. *You coming home with me!* Paranoid, I looked around as if someone could see the drama playing out in my head.

I found an empty seat in the back just as the bus began to pull away from the gate. Tammie was nowhere to be found, but I was far from relaxed and going to sleep was not on my agenda. I carefully watched the time and with every passing hour I would feel a little more relieved. I began to drift off to sleep when a lady came to sit next to me.

"Where you from, Baby" she asked.

Being cautious, I replied, "Maryland."

"I'm Miss Sally, but all the children call me 'Ma Dear'. You can call me that if you want," she said real sweetly.

"Ok," I said.

I AM THE ANCESTOR

She then asked, "What's your name, Sugar?"

"Monique," I replied.

"Well, it's nice to meet you, Monique. Such a pretty girl," she said.

Miss Sally continued to share where she was from and who she was headed to see. She started talking about her boyfriend and how glad she'll be to see him again. She had been up north for about three weeks.

"Where are you going?" she inquired.

I said, "I'm going to Miami!"

Very unexpectedly, she whispered, "You are a runaway."

Boldly, I said, "I'm 18 and I have a diploma. I'm no runaway!"

"You are running away from something. Look," she continued, "you are going to go down there and see that there are men waiting for pretty girls like you because that's all they do. There are men who are looking for boys and girls all the time. They can smell a runaway. Look how cute you are and look at your body. They will abuse you and turn you into a prostitute."

I just sat and listened. *I'm not running away from home, I'm running away from hell.*

Then she changed the subject. "How much money do you have?" she asked.

"I have money for a motel, like $300 to $350," I freely said.

"This is what I am going to do for you: I live by myself, so you can come and stay with me. Give me the money to cover your room and food. Even though I don't' think it will be enough, I'll do this for you, Sugar," she said very nicely.

Without thinking twice, I gave her the money. As I sat looking at Miss Sally, she no longer was just a lady sitting next to me. She was a mother figure, the kind that really cared for a daughter. She appeared to show great concern and wanted to make sure I was not going to be "eaten" by men who waited for naïve girls…like me.

Miss Sally counted the money, stuffed it in her bra, and said, "This will do, Baby." Then, she began to talk about her house and how nice it was. She bragged on her spacious eat-in kitchen and huge porch. She also talked about her yard and how the neighbors tried to get her secret for growing "those lovely tulips." It sounded much better than my home in Baltimore. It sounded very peaceful. Miss Sally was very kind and full of love…something I desperately needed.

The trip to Florida took forever. There were several stops along the way to pick up other passengers and just to rest. We even changed bus driver's once. I ended up sleeping most of the way which helped make the trip a little more tolerable. When we finally arrived, it was the next morning.

I AM THE ANCESTOR

The weather was extremely hot and dry. All I wanted to do was get off of that cramped bus, take a shower, eat, and lie on the bed at my new home.

From the station, we caught a cab to Miss Sally's house. She did not live too far away, luckily. As we drove through town, I saw very nice homes. I kept trying to figure out which belonged to Miss Sally. *Those tulips look like the one's she talked about. Maybe that's her house.* Just as we turned the corner, the cab stopped. Miss Sally gave the driver money, opened the door, and got out.

"Come on, Baby. We're home." she said rather dryly. Then she opened the front door and said, "Your room is right there on the left."

Her home was a shack! It was not at all like she described. There was not a single tulip in her yard. In fact, all I saw were weeds and lots of dandelions. The porch only held two old wooden rocking chairs and the driveway she said her fancy car was parked was nothing but stones with a beat up pick up truck.

When I walked inside, I could see a bedroom with a twin bed while standing in the living room. That was my room. Oh, and her "spacious" eat-in kitchen held nothing more than a little wooden table with one chair. The one level house with no added luxuries was all Miss Sally really had to offer. On top of this, it was really filthy.

I took my bag, went in the room, sat on the bed, and began

to cry. I held onto my duffle bag like it was a teddy bear and eventually cried myself to sleep.

I woke up the next day just to find Miss Sally dressed in a full slip and drunk beyond belief! She started talking but I could not make out any of her words. I just nodded and pretended to understand. This went on for about twenty minutes or so and then she went into her room. Miss Sally really had me fooled on the bus. It appeared that she had it all together as a serious business woman who worked hard to make a living. Not so.

When I saw her fall out on the bed, I shut and locked the front door and went to take a shower. One glance at that bathroom and I knew I had to clean it first. I looked in the kitchen cabinets and in the closet for cleaning supplies. All I found was a broom, dustpan, some bleach, and a rag. That was good enough for me to go to work. I had enough experience working with Tammie cleaning those offices to know that bleach was able to work all by itself. I scrubbed the toilet, sink, tub, and floors like never before. When I was finished, that little bathroom looked brand new!

I had not felt water on my body in close to two days and it showed. I washed from my head to my feet with the bar of soap I packed in my duffle bag. Aside from the soap, my toothbrush, toothpaste, and deodorant, I didn't have time to grab other toiletries before leaving home. I knew I had to get out of there while the getting was good. I did not want to chance Tammie returning and catching me. Even though I wish I had thought my plan through a little more, I was still glad to be gone.

Later on that evening, Miss Sally woke up, took a shower and got dressed. She peeked in my bedroom.

"You cleaned this bathroom, Sugar?" she asked.

I nodded.

"Damn, you good! You want something to eat?" she asked.

Reluctantly, I shook my head even though I was starving. She went to the kitchen and came back to my room with a plate of chicken and potatoes. Looked like something from a restaurant. It didn't matter. I ate that food like it was my last meal.

Miss Sally was making her way back to her room just as someone knocked on the door. It was a group of women and girls about my age who were talking to her about getting a job. She told them that someone would pick them up and take them where they needed to go. After they left, she came to talk to me.

"Monique, I found a job for you to do. Tomorrow, you will go with those women that were just here. They will explain what to do from there," she said.

The next morning I got up and met the group of women across the street. We were all picked up from there and taken to a bus. The bus, which had other people on it already, took us to a part of town where there was nothing but fields and flatlands. Once we got to our destination, I noticed a man standing near a van. There was also a woman there gave us our orders.

"If you are new, get with someone more experienced. Make sure you shadow them so you can learn. Just do exactly as they are doing and work together, now," she said.

I found someone who looked to be experienced and got to work. My team member never gave her name and I never gave mine. There was no talking at all between us. We worked in a field planting sugar cane on our hands and knees all day. I learned what to do through her non-verbal communication. It came in pods and we had to line them row by row. A row could be up to two miles each. We had to break up the soil with a pitchfork, mix lime with the soil and add fertilizer to help the sugar cane grow, drop in the pod, and cover it back with soil. This is what we did all day in the hot Florida sun.

It was now my seventh day in Florida and my fourth day on this job. Once I really got the hang of it, I began to work very hard and very fast. I kept up my usual pace because I wanted to get the work done. Others who worked around me noticed my pace as well and would often say, "Slow it down!" I guess that's one of the good things that came out of working for Tammie. I learned how to work hard for hours at a time.

I AM THE ANCESTOR

 It was still early in the day by the time I was going back to the van to get my next batch of pods. When I got there, the foreman handed the pod batch to another worker waiting behind me and told me to take a ride with him. In my innocence, I jumped in the van. I thought that we were making a pod run since I've seen other females join him on his trips. Boy was I wrong.

The foreman was about 55 years old and very dirty from the work we did. I was dirty, too. He made small talk with me along the way and acted very cordial, too. It put me at ease and did not raise any red flags. He was very nice and gave me no reason to think otherwise. He even told me about his family and that he had a daughter that was about my age who worked at a restaurant. He talked about how proud he was of her and that she was "going to be somebody someday."

Suddenly, he stopped talking and that's when everything changed. Turning the corner, I looked out the window and saw a motel sign. As the van pulled into the parking lot, it dawned on me that this was not a run for more pods. This man was taking me in there to do what had been done to me time and time again. He didn't bother to check in at the front desk. We just went straight to the room, went inside, and closed the door.

As soon as he shut and locked the door, he began undressing. It was disgusting to see all the dirt and filth on his body. My throat was in my chest. I could not speak. He quickly undressed me and had sex with me. I remember laying there lifeless with my eyes closed. The visions of my uncles were there and now this guy would be there, too. I just mentally escaped and forced myself to not remember anything. When he was finished, he got up and put on his clothes. So did I. Once we left the motel, we went to get the pods and drove back to the field. I looked out of the window the entire time and did not say a single word.

We got back to the fields about an hour after we left. I was determined to not say anything to anyone for the rest of the day. I just wanted to finish the job and go home. When my shift was through, I got back in the van with all the others and headed home. One of the girls looked at me rather strangely. I could tell that she knew what happened.

"You went to get the pods, huh?" she said snidely.

I just turned away and looked out of the window.

I got back home to find Miss Sally was not there. I hurried to my bedroom, gathered all my belongings, and left. I walked for what seemed like hours when I came upon a diner on the strip. I could smell the food coming out of the windows. With the little money I had, I went inside to get something to eat. I was very hungry and it showed. Even though people were looking at me, I did not care how much I licked my fingers or smacked my mouth.

Directly across from the diner was a boarding house. It was

very clean on the outside. There was a "Room for Rent" sign hanging on the door so I stopped there. A very tall woman was standing on the porch. She was plainly dressed and her hair was very neat. She reminded me of Helen Willis on "The Jefferson's."

"Hello. Are you looking for a room? I'm Ms. Ridge" she asked.

"Yes. How much does it cost and how often do I have to pay?" I replied.

"Sixty dollars a week," she said.

"I'll take it, Ms. Ridge" I said. I then handed her sixty dollars and she showed me to my room.

Over the next few days, I saw a lot of traffic coming through Ms. Ridge's boarding house. I learned soon enough that she provided housing for prostitutes, mostly. Now and again, she would rent to someone who was temporarily down on their luck. But overall, her tenants were "night walkers."

Around seven o'clock every evening, the girls in the house made their way to the local bar. There, they would have a drink with any man that was offering, and then bring them back to the boarding house to have sex. This was the way the girls paid for the roof over their heads.

Now, one would think that Ms. Ridge was the Madame, but not so. She was strictly a landlord. Whatever her tenants did was their business. She just wanted her money at the beginning of the week. She made all of us pay in advance. That way, she could kick us out immediately if we did not pay on Monday.

I was getting low on funds by the middle of my second week at Ms. Ridge's. I knew that if did not pay her on Monday, I would be out on the streets. No exceptions. Going back to Miss Sally's was not an option and the chances of me finding a decent job that would pay me in the next three days was slim to none. So, I joined the ranks of the other girls and went to the bar.

Based on what I saw the other girls doing, I figured I would walk right into the bar, find a guy, bring him home, have sex, and get my money. Not hardly! I met a guy my first night at the bar, but he did not make a move and I did not know to make a move. The second night I went back, the same thing happened. On the third night I decided to sit at the bar and not a table. I purchased a soda (since I did not drink alcohol) and hoped by doing what others were doing this would invite someone to come my way. Still, no one approached me.

It was now Friday and my money was gone. I returned to the bar anyway and just stood around because I couldn't buy anymore sodas. After walking from one end of the bar to the other, a guy finally approached me.

"How much?" he asked.

I was clueless. I did not know what to say so I just smiled.

"What's your name, Baby?" he continued.

"Robin," I replied.

He said, "OK. Let's go, Robin."

We got in his car and drove back to his place which was not too far from the bar. He was a very handsome and polite guy, making small talk along the way. In my mind, I convinced myself he was my date for the evening. I also begin to think that he would let me stay with him and that I could move out of Ms. Ridges house and all. It was a slick psychological move to take my mind off of what was about to happen. I was cool the entire time and played right along with the game. *It's for your survival, Symbolie.*

When we got to his place, he simply said, "Follow me." He led me to a bedroom, closed the door, and began to undress. I began to undress as well as he watched my every move. His excitement was obvious. Very gently, he pulled me to him and laid me on the bed. Then we had sex. It lasted longer than I wanted it to, but I knew the end would come.

Right after our encounter, he put on his clothes and said, "Your shoes are over there and your coat is over there. Let's go."

He drove me back to the bar and from there I walked back home. We never talked money, but he paid me well. Now, I had enough money to at least pay for my rent come Monday.

This became my new routine for a period of time. Once I got to the point where I had enough money to carry me for a while, I did not go back to the bar. Unlike the majority of the girls in the home, I went only when my money got low. I developed a plan to pay Ms. Ridge at least two weeks in advance so I would not have to scramble for my rent.

Three weeks had gone by and my cash was getting low. I went back to the bar and it took no time for me to catch the attention of a guy on the other side of the bar. From a distance, I could not see his looks. But as he walked toward me he was the ugliest, most beastly man I had ever seen! He, on the other hand, thought he was anything but ugly. He was cocky and sure of himself, dressed to a "T", and was holding lots of money in his hand.

"Hey, Baby. You got time?" he asked.

I simply nodded.

"Come on. Let's get out of here," he said.

I was frightened beyond belief, but I went anyway. I needed money.

We went somewhere other than his house. He made sure that I knew. Wasting no time, he started making freaky and sickening statements as he undressed. He seemed very sure of himself and claimed to have "much skill" when it came to women. I never gave him eye contact and did not talk.

I AM THE ANCESTOR

However, as I began undressing slowly, the tone of his voice changed and so did his confidence.

"Women don't like me. I'm always nice to them though. I don't treat them mean like those other men at the bar and I do it to them gently. I never did nothing mean to nobody. I keep money, too. They just don't like me," he said.

The room was very dim. He took his keys and his wallet out of his pockets and placed them on the table as I continued to undress. When he glanced at me unbuttoning my shirt, he got ready...I mean really ready! I got scared all over again and knew I could not have sex with that man. Without warning my thoughts shifted. *Get out, Girl!* As he turned to climb on the bed, I grabbed his keys and wallet and ran like never before!

"You bitch," he yelled. "Get your ass back here with my shit," he continued.

I ran all the way back to the boarding house and stayed there and hoped he would not find me. When I got in my room, I counted the money in his wallet. I had hit the jackpot. I never returned to the bar again.

Ms. Ridge came to me many nights later and said, "You've been hanging here a lot lately. You going out tonight or do you plan to stay here with me?"

"I am going to stay home tonight, Ms. Ridge," I replied.

"Well, there is going to be an overnight crew coming

through in a few hours and I think you are the boss' type," she said, smiling.

"Okay," I replied and went to my room to prepare for the evening guests.

When night came, eight guys came to the house. I have seen many men come and go, but I've never seen this group of men at Ms. Ridge's. They were very big, obviously strong, and lively but not in a rude way. One guy was dressed cleanly and wore very nice cologne. I knew immediately he was the boss Ms. Ridge spoke of earlier. Then there was a man who appeared to be the body guard. He looked like a Native American and was as big as a Sumo wrestler. He stood behind the leader the entire time and went wherever he went...even to the bathroom. Taha was his name. The other six guys were just a part of the crew.

Taha was a very interesting guy. He reminded me of that big slimy looking character on Star Wars. He had a very large cut over his right eye that caused it to be partially closed. His choice of clothing was rather interesting as well. He wore a black leather vest, black slacks, and black motorcycle boots. He always wore a black scarf around his neck. Apparently, he had gotten stabbed there, too, some time ago and used the scarf to hide the wound. Because he only wore a vest, the stab and bullet wounds on his arms were very large. From time to time while he stood next to the boss, he would twirl his finger around the hole that was in his wrist. It disgusted me to see him do this.

Ms. Ridge took me and the men to a back room that I had never seen before. From the outside it looked like a book case, but when she slid them apart it actually covered a set of doors that led to another room. There was a small bar, two tables, eight chairs, and one barstool there. Four of the six guys set up two tables and joined them together. One was needed for a game of cards. The other was to hold their bags of drugs and money...and there was plenty of both!

Once we were all inside, Ms. Ridge told me to sit on the stool and not to move. I looked at her, sat on the stool, and then she left. The boss, who was never called by name, gestured for me to come to him. Nervous on the inside but calm on the outside, I walked over to him right away. Before he spoke, he raised his left hand and Taha took about three steps back but kept his eyes on me the entire time and began breathing very hard.

"Go over to that table and bring me back that black bag," he said.

I did exactly as he asked and Taha moved back in his spot behind the boss. As I was returning to give it to him, the boss raised his left hand again and Taha stepped back once more but kept his eyes glued to me. The boss reached out his hand while looking me straight in my eyes. It was very strange, but I did not give it much thought. I gave him the black bag and then returned to the stool near the wall and stayed there for about three hours.

The men drank and played cards late into the night. No one touched the drugs and only the boss and Taha were sober.

"Enough," the boss said. Then he raised his right hand.

Taha looked at the other men and simply said, "Go." Immediately the men all left and went to the rooms where the girls were waiting for them. Taha then looked at me and said, "You, too." I did just as he said.

I was exhausted, hot, and sweaty. I decided to take a shower and then go back to my room and wait for the boss. He came into my room minutes later and found me in my underwear. This time, Taha was not with him and God knows I was so glad about that. I stood there frozen a bit not knowing if I should put on the rest of my clothes or just take off my panties. I decided to not do either and just sat on my mattress on the floor.

The boss slowly walked over to where I was and sat down next to me. I was so nervous I was shaking. I couldn't even look at him. All I could think about was how I saw bosses portrayed in the movies and how rough and mean they were. I didn't know what he was going to do to me.

I stayed on the mattress and looked straight ahead. Out of the corner of my eye, I could see that he was looking me over. He did so for a very long time and did not speak a word. Then, he began to rub my back, but his touch was different. He did not rub me the way other men did before having sex with them. It was a feeling I had never felt before.

"I've been watching you, Girl. You should not be here," he said. "I don't know how in the hell you got yourself here."

I had no idea what was about to happen. I was terrified, but I did not move and I did not speak. The boss continued talking.

"You sat in that room for hours while I was playing cards and not once did you ask to cop any of the bags like everybody else did. I knew right then that you just didn't belong here. The more I look at you, the more it's like looking at my kids, baby sister, or nieces. There is no way that I can do anything with your ass. Shit! I've even lost my dick to mess with one of the other girls, damn it," he said under his breath a bit.

I started crying and shaking again. He wiped my eyes and gave me a hug from the side.

"Get up and get dressed," he said. I moved right away and put on a pair of jeans, a bra, and a shirt.

What happened next actually changed my life forever. The boss reached in his pocket and gave me a knot of money without even counting it as if he already knew the amount.

"Take this and put it in a bag that you carry every day," he said. "Don't you let nobody know I gave it to you, you hear?"

I nodded and did exactly as he said.

He sat back down on the mattress.

"Come here," he said.

Again, I obeyed and sat back down beside him. He continued talking to me.

"In the morning, I'm going to pretend to send you to the store. Don't bring your ass back here. I'm telling you: don't come back!" he whispered.

"OK," I said, as tears began to roll down my cheek again.

"Stop crying, Baby," he said. "You look just like my daughters. Damn it! This is so unreal; it just ain't right, Girl."

The boss hugged me for a very long time. I hugged him back just as long. Never in my life had I ever felt protected like that. Never in my life had I been protected like that. God used a stranger to rescue me from hell.

He looked at me once more and said, "Lay down...on your side."

I climbed in the bed to lie on my side. The boss got in the bed behind me but did not press his body against mine. It was the weirdest thing I had ever experienced. *Love must feel like this*. He gently continued rubbing my arms as I began falling asleep.

I AM THE ANCESTOR

It was very quiet. I could tell that Taha was standing outside of the door because I could hear his breathing. I guess he went to be with one of the other girls first and then came back to work for the boss. I was getting very tired and began drifting off to sleep. The boss continued to rub my arms. The last thing I heard him say as I was dozing off was, "You getting out of this shithole."

The next morning, the boss woke me up about nine o'clock.

"Go take a shower and get dressed. Don't play around, either. Hurry back," he ordered.

I moved quickly and returned back to the room.

"Leave your bag here for now. You can get it when I send you to the store. Let's go," he said.

As we made our way to the door, he stopped, turned around and looked me straight in my eyes, and gave me a very strong hug. He then kissed me on both of my cheeks and opened the door.

Making our way downstairs, we noticed Ms. Ridge was cooking breakfast. The boss and I went to sit at the table.

"Ridgey," he said. "You got any fresh garlic? I need to chew on some before I eat breakfast."

Ms. Ridge looked in the refrigerator, turned to him and said, "I sure don't, Boss."

"Come here, Girl," he said to me.

I got up and went to him.

"Take this money and go to the market and get me some fresh garlic. Make sure it's pure white, too," he said as he looked me in my eyes and pressed the money in my hand.

"OK, Boss," I replied.

I placed the money in my pocket and got up from the table. I went back upstairs to get my bag and then walked out of the door. I walked in the direction of the store, but took a quick detour to go to the bus stop. Nervously, I waited for about ten minutes before one came. Then, I got on the bus and headed straight for the Greyhound station, praying the entire time that no one would see me.

When I finally got there, I heard the announcer say, "Now boarding at gate 22 for Hartford, CT."

That's all I needed. With some money I already had saved, I went to the counter, got my ticket, and boarded that bus. I never returned to Florida.

My mind was spinning around and around. Off and on during my trip back up north, I tried to make sense of what just happened. I replayed in my mind my brief time in Florida and all the life lessons I had learned. It was clear to me that I would do at least three things differently this time once I arrived in Connecticut:

I AM THE ANCESTOR

1. I will not give my money to anybody.

2. I will live in a motel.

3. I will find a job.

I feel it's necessary to stop here and just have a moment to confess. Considering all of the abuse I suffered, I never imagined being in a position whereby I would have to give my body away to survive. What my uncles did to me was shameful, no doubt. However, having to live my life as a prostitute was just as shameful.

At times, it saddens me to think that for the first 21 years of my life my body did not really belong to me. It was either taken against my will to satisfy the sick needs of other people or given away against my desire to do so in order to keep food in my mouth, clothes on my back, and shelter over my head. The mental pain that I went through as a result of both of those instances haunted me for years to come. I'm glad to say that I have let those bad memories go and have moved on in my life.

The next day, I arrived in Connecticut. I got off the bus and immediately found a restroom. I didn't really have to go, I just wanted to count the money the boss gave me. I went in the biggest stall I could find. First, I pulled out the money he gave me for "the garlic". It was a fifty dollar bill. Then, I grabbed the knot of money in my bagged. It was a total of

$1500! I nearly screamed! Quickly, I stuffed the money way back down in my bag and left.

Things moved pretty quickly once I got in Hartford. I found a motel not too far from the bus station and found a job as a Security Guard within weeks of arriving. I worked that job for one year and, of course, was a top performing employee. Eventually, I was able to move out of the motel and into a very nice efficiency. Life was great and, for the first time in years, I had stability…and peace. Things were really starting to look up for me.

During my lunch break one day, I decided to read the "Classified" section of the paper. There, I saw an ad for the Police Academy. It got my attention so I called to get more details. Because I worked from 6 a.m. to 2 p.m., I was able to apply for the academy the same day after my shift ended. *Let's see how this goes.*

No more than a month later I received a letter congratulating me on the acceptance of my application into the academy and that I was scheduled for the written exam. I was pumped! The following month, I took the written exam and received another letter of congratulations stating that I passed and was scheduled for the oral exam. Two weeks later, I took and passed the oral exam and was then scheduled to take a physical and polygraph test. I aced those as well.

I cannot begin to describe how amazed I was. It was not

that long before that I was on the run, ended up in Florida, prostituted to keep a roof over my head and food on my table, and then suddenly turned my life around with the help of a stranger who treated me like his little sister. I knew that it was God protecting me.

The final part of the application process into the Police Academy was fingerprinting. On the appointment letter I received in the mail, it stated that I would need two forms of identification, preferably a photo ID and a birth certificate. *Oh no! Not again.* And so it was that for the first time since I left home I would have to call Tammie. I had not spoken to her in over two years and to not speak to her for another two or twenty-two years would have been fine with me. Nevertheless, I had to make contact if I expected to get my birth certificate.

I did not waste any time calling home. My grandmother answered the phone.

"Hello," she said.

"Hi, Grandma. It's Bolie," I responded.

"Hey, Baby," she said. "Remember the night you left and you said 'Goodbye'? I knew that you were leaving."

I did not know what to say to her, so I just asked for Tammie. When she got to the phone, I went straight to the point.

"Mom, I passed the test to become Police Officer. I need my birth certificate," I said, directly.

She asked, "Where are you?"

"Mom, I passed the physical exam and the oral and written test. Did you file for my birth certificate yet?" I asked.

"There you go with that shit again," she shouted. "You need to come home. This is where you belong...right here with us," she said.

"Mom, did you get it?" I asked, wondering if that was the reason she said I need to come home.

"You should just come home, Bolie," she replied very calmly. Never did she tell me whether or not she got my birth certificate.

The fear I felt for years when I lived with her came rushing back. In an instant, I become that little girl who did whatever her mother said do or run the risk of being beat lifeless. Tammie had absolutely no idea where I was and probably no way to find out. Nevertheless, I was so trained to obey her every word that I did not think to tell her "No" and just hang up the phone.

Instead, I replied, "Yes, Ma'am," and hung up the phone.

I was twenty-one years old.

EIGHT

The Only Place I Know to Call Home

I SAT IN MY RECLINING CHAIR LIMP, REFLECTING ON WHAT just happened. My mind took me back to what caused me to leave Baltimore to how life was at that moment. Although Hartford was a much better place, I reasoned my life was not going the way I wanted and I just needed to go back home. Life with Tammie and my family was the only consistency I knew with all its abuse and pain. Within a week, I gave my landlord back the keys, quit my job, and headed back to Baltimore leaving behind my dreams of a career with the police department.

Most of my family greeted me with a hug and a smile and said they missed me. Uncle Horace was included in these expressions. Uncle Samuel and Uncle Roger kept their distance. If they had thought about putting their hands on me, I would have moved to the other side of the room. The thought of their hands touching me made me sick to my stomach. It was a bitter sweet feeling when I greeted them in return because of all the people there, Uncle Horace and my grandmother were the only two I was truly glad to see.

My family never knew where I was while I was gone for the four years. No one asked me where I went or how I survived. Someone once told me that they saw an ad in the Afro Sun about a missing 17 year old that was being searched for at the time. I have never seen proof of that article. For all I know it could be hearsay because at the time I was 18 years old. But, Tammie could have placed the ad and lied about my age to get more attention. If she used 17 years old then technically I would have been considered a child and priority would have been given to the case.

The entire family moved to another house a little bit smaller than the one I left. It was both rat and roach infested. More people were living there now. Many of my cousins and their children made it overcrowded. They had lost gotten evicted from their homes because they did not pay their rent. That had nothing to do with them not having the money, most of the time. They just chose to spend it gambling, drinking, or drugging. When evening came, every corner of the house became a bedroom. Makeshift doors and curtains, draped from one end of the wall to the other, were set up to provide as much privacy as possible. Reluctantly, I stayed in the room with Tammie.

It did not take me long to get a job. As soon as Tammie saw I was back in position and bringing home money on a steady basis, she made her move.

"We should get out of here. Between the two of us, we can do better than this, Bolie. I've had enough of their shit and I want out," she said.

It was fine with me to go along with her plan. In fact, I was glad to move out because Uncle Samuel had not changed a bit. His girlfriend moved in with us, but that did not stop him from making harassing comments and gestures. Although he never touched me again, he made sure to mention that I had "gotten all grown up" every time he saw me. *You can look, but you better not touch!*

A month passed before Tammie found a place. She insisted that I give my checks directly to her so she could cash them. I did just as she said. Although she appeared to have mellowed out and may have even thought twice about beating me, she was still my mother and I made sure to respect and obey her. I knew no other way.

We had a very decent apartment and our relationship was cordial. There were no confrontations and there were no beatings. She worked just as hard as I did while still doing odd jobs in between. Because our shifts sometimes overlapped, we would barely see each other which did not bother me at all. For once, I felt that we were establishing the bond that I had longed for all of my life. That we were finally going to be mother and daughter. By all appearances, things were going well!

Tammie and I came and went as we pleased. Whenever I decided to hang out, she would typically ask where I was going and what time I would return home. She rarely questioned me beyond that and never enforced a curfew. For the first time in my life, I felt free from Tammie's controlling ways. I was an adult. Finally, I was grown!

Then, it happened. One Saturday night as I was making my way out of the door, Tammie was coming in from working her night shift. Without warning, she went into a rage.

"I'm sick and tired of you running in and out of this house all hours of the night. I can't sleep with all the noise from that damn alarm clock of yours and the fucking phone ringing off the hook," she screamed.

I stood there looking at her for about ten seconds. I was just getting ready to say something back to Tammie, but decided to just walk out the door. I went to the bus stop around the corner and just sat there for a minute. Then, I began to replay bits and pieces of my life as a child and then as a runaway. One thought to the other reminded me of nothing but pain and I was not about to suffer anymore

"I'm a grown woman, not a child! I've been through too much shit in my life to deal with anymore of her mess," I said out loud as tears welled up in my eyes. *I'm outta there!*

I AM THE ANCESTOR

Three days later, I was gone.

I found an apartment close to my job. Not having transportation prevented me from moving too far away. But, I knew it was only a matter of time before I saved enough money to get a car. I filled out the application and worked out a deal with the rental company to just pay the security deposit. I promised to pay the first month's rent within two weeks when I got paid and I did.

I still had most of my items at the apartment Tammie and I shared. I knew had to go back and get my things or else she would sell, giveaway, or trash my belongings. A month later when I knew she would not be home, I went back, packed all of my stuff, and left the room clean and bare. A friend, who drove me there, helped me load my stuff in her car. Once we took out the last bit of my items, I threw my key back inside the house, and pulled the door shut.

My newfound peace mirrored what I felt while living in Hartford. Over the next several months, I was able to fully decorate my apartment and make it feel like a real home. I also purchased a used car and started dating a guy who worked for a office supply store. Before I could blink, we were in a pretty serious relationship which led to me getting pregnant. Almost immediately, things started changing. It seemed like he picked arguments with me constantly. By the end of my first trimester, he was no where to be found. I knew it was only a matter of time.

The way he rolled out without warning was painful, but it was nothing I couldn't handle. Suffering for one reason or another was old news for me. I would often remember what Ms. Ridge told me one day before I was heading to the bar: "What don't kill you will make you stronger." I was determined to focus all of my attention on my unborn child and make sure that I would be the best mom he or she ever had because it was something I never had! There were no other choices in the matter.

While preparing to visit the doctor's for a routine checkup one afternoon, I received a call from Uncle Horace. He told me that Uncle Samuel had died suddenly. I was stunned, but felt no sadness at all and did not ask any questions. Instead, I cancelled my appointment and went straight to his girlfriend's house to share my condolences.

Crying, she said, "I don't know what happened. We were having sex and all of sudden he started coughing up blood. Then, blood started shooting out of his penis."

I was speechless as I stood there rubbing her back. *That bastard got what he deserved! He died as he lived: with his dick in his hand!*

If ever you want to see someone you have not seen in a long time, just go to a funeral. To my pleasant surprise, Frank was there. I had not seen him in over eleven years. He looked really good, although he was balding a bit on top.

I AM THE ANCESTOR

We hugged for a very long time and he gave me the biggest kiss ever. We sat with each other during the repast, but did not do much talking. Afterwards he walked me to my car. It was then that he struck up a conversation…one that I will never forget.

"I want to talk to you for a minute, Baby," he said.

I said, "Yes, Sir!"

"I only came to the funeral for one reason and one reason only," he continued.

I just looked at him and allowed him to talk. He had the most serious look on his face and appeared to have a sense of urgency in his tone.

"Remember when you were in the hospital and I never came to see you? Well, you were not in the hospital because of me," he said.

Confused, I replied, "Daddy, I don't know why I was in the hospital at all."

Frank took a deep sigh, shook his head, and began to speak once more.

"He said, "Bolie, you were in the hospital because you were near death with a sexually transmitted disease. At the time, I did not know but I later found out from your grandmother. Tammie told me not to go see you because you had a urinary tract infection and that you would be uncomfortable.

But, I still wanted to see you because you were my little girl, Sweetheart."

I began to cry but wiped my tears away quickly. I folded my arms and dropped my head so Frank would not see me cry. I always wondered why he never came to visit me. For a very long time, I thought that he did not love me anymore or that he felt I was a bad little girl because I had gotten sick and put in the hospital. Well, it looked like I was about to find out the truth.

"Tammie also told me that the doctors would have to keep your gown lifted all the time to check you and make sure you were drying out from the infection. She knew the type of man I was and that I would not come in the room if you were naked like that. Bolie, that's why I didn't come to visit.. But, it does not stop there. I didn't find out until later that when the doctors and social workers asked bout your condition, Tammie told them that her husband...me...had been touching you and having sex with you and that was why you had what you had. She also told them that I was not your real father and she asked me to leave the home. And that's the God's honest truth, Baby."

The only word I could get out of my mouth was, "What?" I leaned on my car the entire time he talked. I tried to speak, but my mind began reeling. One flashback after another jumped around in my head and I began to cry even more. Frank grabbed me and hugged me like he had never hugged me before. All he could say was, "I'm sorry, Baby Girl. I'm so sorry."

The rest of the family began to file out of the dining hall and my eyes immediately fixed on Tammie. My thoughts of her were that of the lowest person that ever walked the earth. *How could she be so cruel and evil? How could she literally destroy someone's life the way she did Frank's?*

It was a fact that, during the time all of this went down, Tammie never bothered to ask if anyone had touched me. Not once did she say, "Bolie, is there anything you want to tell me?" If she knew after all these years why would she let it continue to happen? Why did she let them molest and rape me over and over from the time I was four up until I ran away from home? What type of monster was she? She was the type that knew all along what was going on and did not do a damn thing to help me.

Just as Tammie began walking towards us, Frank gave me one final kiss and walked away. She stood just a few feet away from me watching him walk in and out of cars and then around the corner.

"You alright?" she asked.

I looked her straight in the eyes and said, "I'm better than I've ever been in my entire life."

I then got in my car, started it up, and drove away.

NINE

In it to Win it; My Purpose

CAN'T REALLY EXPLAIN WHY, BUT AFTER MY UNCLE DIED I felt free. I began to believe that I was so much more than the abuse I had suffered. With new life on the inside and memories of my old life buried six feet under, a brand new day was dawning. It's really amazing how I never really noticed the cloud that hung over my head all those years until I began to see the sunshine!

I was truly an independent woman determined to provide the best life possible for myself and my soon to be born child. My entire pregnancy was without complications. I rolled into my ninth month like a champ and continued to work as a dedicated employee right up to the day I delivered my daughter Courtney. She was the most beautiful, round baby girl I had ever seen in my entire life. And she was mine because I always wanted to be a mom! Everything I did from that moment on was because of that. I made a promise to Courtney that I was going to be the best mom she had ever had and along the way show my mom how to be a mom!

Courtney was a joy to have. She was a very peaceful child who was not hard to please. Whenever we were out, people would say, "What a quiet child you have. Hardly know she's there!" She really only cried when she was wet or hungry. I loved dressing her in cute little dresses and lace sock. There was never a day she did not have ponytails and I always made time to take her to story time at the library. When she began attending school, I spent time in her classroom during my lunch break everyday. I was very helpful to her teachers and was often called "The Classroom Mom."

Courtney did not waste anytime learning whatever I tried to teach her. An extremely bright child, she was potty trained by the time she was one year old and reading by the time she was two years old. I strongly encourage any mother to expose their child to the library at an early age. It is really a great resource to make a part of their young life.

I managed my home and my finances to a "T". My weekly budget helped me to live below my means and kept me on course financially. I only spent out of necessity and banked the rest. My savings grew quickly and I used the money to help me buy my first house. Growing up in Baltimore with the family I had, no one owned a house. We just rented them and when we could not pay the rent, we just left and moved into another house. I was living life in a way my family had never dreamed and it was all good!

When Courtney was about four years old, I began to casually date a young man from Baltimore named Christopher Belkerson. I liked his distinguished name. It was clear that he was not interested in marriage and I was fine with that. Christopher owned a small business and worked extremely hard to make it successful. We casually dated for about three months even though I knew he was not ready for a serious relationship. Ready or not, I became pregnant. This time I had a gorgeous chocolate baby boy. Naturally, I named him Christopher, Jr. Now, things were perfect! I had Courtney, my sweet little girl, and Christopher, my handsome baby boy.

I dreamt of braiding his thick hair, buying him his first puppy, and signing him up for basketball or football or both. I thought about the strength of his name...and that no one could or would change it! I was determined to not let anybody call him "Chris" or "CJ". He had to be called Christopher to show the strength in his name. And I would call him Master Belkerson!

I was going to raise him to be a bold leader who would stand up for what was right. He would protect his big sister the best he could and not let anyone get over on her. He was the "man cub" that I always wanted and believed I would have. Whether or not his father helped out or spent time with him, he was going to be raised the right way. He was going to be respectful of all people, given the same opportunities to learn as his sister, and loved unconditionally by his mother.

Courtney and Christopher got along so well. There was never any real sibling rivalry and one would always look out for the other. Onlookers would compliment me on how well my children looked and how well mannered they were. I made sure I kept Courtney's hair freshly done and Christopher met with his barber weekly. They wore color coordinated outfits when it was time for family pictures, went to birthday parties together, and shared with each other most of the time. When it came to his trucks, Christopher drew the line.

With two children depending on me to provide for them, I found a more prestigious job at a very reputable company that paid me more money. Tammie who was still in the picture here and there hated to see that I was doing so well. She would make jealous comments that I was "popping out those kids like popcorn" and that as far as she was concerned she only had grandchildren. I guess that was her way of disowning me. Because she never really made me feel like I belonged, I was not missing too much.

Nevertheless, I did not let her foolishness bother me at all. After everything I had experienced, I could have ended up strung out on drugs, still prostituting, or even dead. I was not about to let that happen. Instead, I stayed on course, took care of my children, and continued to position myself well on my job. Close to every six months, I earned some type of promotion, merit, or certificate for one accomplishment or another. I knew my stuff (and others, too) and was a serious team player. Whatever I had to share, I shared. Whatever I learned, I taught others. In essence, what was mine was theirs.

Strangely enough, after earning the biggest bonus of my career, my desire to become an entrepreneur began to pique. I figured if I worked this hard for somebody else then I need to do the same thing for myself. I wanted to run a business that would support young mothers like me but didn't know quite where to start. So, I went to the yellow pages and found the telephone number for the Small Business Administration and gave them a call.

The man on the phone suggested that I enroll in a class on owning and operating a business. Without hesitation, I did. I was very focused on learning everything I could and then some. Although my schedule was already full with work, children, and a few activities for myself, I could not let that stop me. I factored this class into the equation, removed the "fluff", and made it work. After completing the six week course, I graduated and received a certificate. Things were really moving along great!

Next, I developed a business plan, built a portfolio that I knew would come in handy when applying for loans, and began building a relationship with various banks. Once those relationships became more and more established, I submitted various applications for loans and other forms of assistance. Lastly, I sought out commercial locations for the business, researched insurance requirements, and submitted my bond application.

By the time all was said and done, I used my savings for every possible start up cost imaginable. The steps I had to take were now checked off of my list. Just four months earlier, I walked into my first class not knowing anything at all about running a business. But I did what I could to educate myself along the way by reading books and attending two more classes. Now, I felt confident and equipped to not only start my business but also to run it just as effectively as a Fortune 500 company. Now, I was ready!

TEN

Declined...Rejected...Can't Help You

DEAR SYMBOLIE SMITH,

We regret to inform you that your application for a bond is being declined for the following reasons...

The text that followed is a blur to me now. I only remember there were notes written in the "For Office Use Only" section and the signature of one Ms. Brown. In essence, the letter stated that my documentation was invalid. I immediately went back to my check list and reviewed all of the steps I took. My notes clearly stated that I submitted my driver's license and social security card as identification, so I was confused about what they meant by "invalid."

The next day I called and inquired about why I was declined. Clearly, I dotted every "I" and crossed every "T". I needed clarification, so I called Ms. Brown

"Hello. My name is Symbolie Smith and I'm calling about a

decline letter I received. I need some information, please," I said.

"OK, Ms. Smith. Read the five digit code in the gray box on the bottom right hand side for me, please," she replied.

Once I read the code to Ms. Brown, she stated that my application was declined due to inconsistencies with my social security number. Once an inconsistency is found, the application process is halted and declined. I explained to Ms. Brown that the number I gave on the application was the number I used when filing other forms. Considering there was nothing she could do and that she did not have specific information, I had to investigate the problem myself.

Before called anyone, I called Tammie to find out about the birth certificate once more. For more than five years I asked her for that piece of paper and she had yet to give it to me. I dialed her number, let the phone ring twice, and then quickly hung up the phone. I changed my mind because in my gut I knew going to her would only make matters worse. I recalled past confrontations and could not count on her to help. I decided, instead, to get on the computer and search for answers myself.

Day and night, I typed my name, social security number, and date of birth hoping to find something, hoping to get answers. In the meantime, I sent countless letters with copies of my identification and requested copies of all documents bearing my name. I even went to the department of social services in downtown Baltimore to see if they could help. They stated there was nothing they could give me since I was not born in the state of Maryland. I had to request a copy of all original applications from my birthplace - the state of New York.

On top of every letter I sent from that point forward, I used what I felt would be an eye catching statement:

"I don't know who I am, can anyone help me, PLEASE!"

I told them I did not have a copy of my birth certificate because Tammie would not release it to me and the chances of me getting a copy from her were slim to none. I recounted the story of being accepted into the police academy but not being able to move forward because I had no identification. I told them about how well I did in those business start-up classes but that my bond application was declined. I pleaded with them for help and to just pro-vide me with copies of the original applications of my social security card and birth certificate. I always closed my letters telling them there assistance would help me tremendously.

I waited for weeks at a time hoping to hear a positive response. Not so. Every government office I contacted replied that my information was inconsistent. Under the name Symbolie Monique Smith were at least three different social security numbers. One particular social security num-ber showed two different names for Tammie. And where

I AM THE ANCESTOR

Tammie's name was correct, mine had a different last name or middle name. On top of this, there were different places of birth and even different races! *Who am I? WHAT am I?*

That was the last straw. I got on the phone and called Tammie. I had enough and was ready for her. This time, all niceties went out the door. I was furious!

"Hello?" she answered.

"What is this? All these years I've been asking for my birth certificate, trying to make a decent life for me and my children, and I find out not only are my names messed up but I might not even be 100% Black? Tell me something!" I screamed.

She said, "You are really getting on my nerves! You are so damn ungrateful, Bolie."

I could not believe she said that!

"Ungrateful? Ungrateful for what? All the beatings, all the lies, all the abuse? Do you really expect a 'Thank You' from me after you almost got me killed by not stopping your brothers from raping me? What, do you expect gratitude for locking me in my room as blood ran down my arm or making me share a room with Aunt Shelly and deal with her crying day and night after you made her get rid of her baby? Grateful? For what, Mommy? The two by four you used to knock me around? Never mind I'm paying for you to have electricity running through your house at this very moment. Never mind that when you need me I'm always there for you in spite of you nearly killing me a few times. Ungrateful? For what, Mommy?" I asked.

I tried to stop, but the thought of that piece of wood banging my little body would not let me.

"Did it ever occur to you that I could have beat you like you beat me a long time ago? Well, I could have. Believe it or not, I never once thought about laying a hand on you. I never wanted to do you harm because I loved you. I never, ever dishonored you or disrespected you. There were people in our family that would tell me to beat you and even kill you. They even said they would help. But, I'm not cruel like that. I am not evil like you. I have a heart and I have a soul and I would never do that to you. But, because of what you have done for me, you will pay. My Creator will make sure of that. So, I don't have to do anything but sit back and watch," I said.

I could hear her breathing getting very heavy. She didn't say anything for a while. Then she spoke.

"I wonder sometimes where I would be if I had been nurtured. How much better of a life I would have and so would you. The moment you took me, you became my "mother", but there was never a connection. Do you realize I have never gotten a birthday card from you? Whatever happened to reading me a story before I went to bed? If you had done that, I would not feel the need to go to book club gatherings every now and again and sit quietly while the other adults read the book. We have not shared a Mother's Day or any other day together for as long as I've been alive," I said.

"Look—you should just stop calling me about this. I'm tired of talking about this shit," she yelled. Then, very calmly she said, "I'm going to go to my grave with you being a gift from God."

Then, she hung up the phone.

Rage consumed me! Every possible unhealthy emotion caused my body to shake. I was through with Tammie while mad at myself. I knew it was going to be a waste of time talking to her. I knew she was going to dodge the issue and not do what she said she would do. All the years she claimed to have called this place, and wrote the place for my birth certificate was nothing but a big fat lie!

I picked up the phone again. This time, I called my grandmother. I told her that there seems to be something strange going on with my birth papers and I needed her help.

Whispering, my grandmother replied, "Baby, she hasn't told you yet? Oh, Lord. She should have told you by now," she said slightly.

"Tell me what by now, Grandma?" I asked firmly.

She responded, "I don't know, Bolie. She just showed up with you one day."

"Grandma, what do you mean 'showed up with me'?" I asked.

Nervously, my grandmother said, "Baby, I gotta go now. Talk to Lee." Then she hung up the phone.Lee is the wife of another uncle of mine named Teddy. Uncle Teddy is the most stable of all of my grandparent's children. He and Lee have been married for over 16 years. He has always been a very strong family man who really takes care of his four children. He drove a tractor trailer and typically visited my grandmother during the holidays. Uncle Teddy has never done anything to hurt me in any way.

I called to speak with Lee and learned that my uncle was home at the time, too. So, I had a chance to talk to both of them.

The first thing my uncle told me was he lived with Tammie in New York for about a year between 1967 and 1968. Tammie lived alone at the time and did not have me. He then moved back to Baltimore in late 1968. Around 1969, he went back to visit Tammie for about a month and she was living with a guy named Ricky. Still, there was no sign of me. He left again and did not return until the summer of 1970 and there I was. Tammie told my uncle weird stories about my biological mother. One thing she said was my biological mother was Spanish looking and had too many kids so she gave me to Tammie. My uncle said that Tammie's story did not sound right at the time, but because she was "the crazy type" he just listened to her.

I AM THE ANCESTOR

Lee got on the phone at that point. She told me that she never visited New York while my uncle lived there. All the stories she heard about me came straight from my Uncle Teddy. That was all they knew.

I thanked them both for their time, hung up the phone, and sat there for a moment. My head was spinning. Then, I had a thought: if my grandmother and my uncle had information, then there had to be others who knew something too. I immediately thought of my Uncle Samuel's girlfriend, Nicole, and gave her a call. Nicole said she didn't know much, but heard my uncle and Tammie fussing one day about me. Then, she heard him say, "You fucking stole that girl and you know it." Nicole said she later asked my uncle what was going on between him and Tammie and why he said Tammie stole me. All he said then was, "That bitch is crazy."

"Symbolie, I believe that Tammie took you from somebody in New York because she never said anything to any of us about being pregnant, the hospital, or nothing like that. I think your uncle knew about this, too, and would use it against her whenever he had a chance. She would give him money anytime he asked even though she didn't want to. And, out of all of her brothers, he was the only one who ever won in an argument with her. For some strange reason, she would just back down from him," Nicole said.

A sharp pain jumped through my stomach. It was not strange at all for Tammie to back down from Uncle Samuel. It did not take much for me to piece together that the reason why Tammie never said anything to anyone about Uncle Samuel molesting me and raping me was because he knew she stole me. She even overlooked the obvious passion marks he would put on my neck! If she said anything to him about what he was doing to me or if she told the police, he would tell the police that she stole me from New York. Tammie sold my soul for the sake of her freedom.

"Do you know anybody else that might have some information about me?" I asked, desperately.

"I sure do. Call your Uncle Pete and Ms. Minnie. They went to New York when Tammie was there more than any of us. They might know something. Good luck, Girl," she said.

I hung up from Nicole and called my Uncle Pete first. Like my Uncle Teddy, Uncle Pete never wronged me. For most of my young years, he was in jail. When he was not in jail, he stayed in the streets. On a few occasions he actually went to NY to visit Tammie. He told me that he met my biological mother once. Tammie had taken him to her apartment not too far away from where she lived. He said he never would forget because it was cluttered and he could barely make his way inside the door. He also said he remembered seeing about five or six other children in the place. They were barely dressed and did not look clean at all.

"Baby, I hope you find out everything you need to know. Don't make no damn sense that your mother won't tell you nothing. One day, she is going to pay for all the shit she did to you. Just you wait and see. She's gonna pay," he said.

Then, we said goodbye.

The last person I called was Ms. Minnie, a good friend of the family. She would drop by the house from time to time, mostly to visit my grandmother. There were times when she would hang out with Tammie, but it was not that often. She even visited ammie a time or two in New York. She said that they would always go to a bar up the street from the apartment. Tammie would meet this Spanish looking lady there and they would drink for hours.

"Her name was something like Mary or Margaret or Mattie... something like that. I knew it was with a "M" because my name starts with a "M". That's why it's so easy to remember," she said.

She did not know anything else, but said that if there was anything else she could do for me to let her know. I told her I would.

My head was beginning to hurt from all of the conversations I had. Within an hour, I learned more about my past than I had ever known. I wrote everything in a book that I kept in my purse at all times.

About twenty minutes later, my phone rang. It was my Uncle Roger calling and he was very upset. Apparently, he heard I was asking people in my family what was going on and why Tammie could not produce a real birth certificate for me.

"It was strange the way she came in the house with you that day. Tammie couldn't even say your name right," he said, obviously upset.

"Don't get mad, Uncle. I just need a few answers. Can I ask you some questions?" I asked.

"Sure, Bolie," he said.

"Do you know anything about me and my past?" I asked.

"I only went to New York one time to visit Tammie. I would only know the area by sight. Based on what I remember, Tammie kept telling us that she was keeping you for her friend. Whenever we asked her for your name, she would pronounce it but we still did not understand her. She never showed us any papers on you. When we asked her to write it down, she refused. So, we asked to see your papers but she never had any. So, because I wanted to make sure you had a name, I told her to tell me one more time. Then, I wrote down what I thought she was saying – Cimbowly, Simbale, Cymbolay Symbolie – and picked the name that closely related to the way it sounded. That's how we got 'Symbolie'," he replied.

"What else, Uncle?" I pleaded.

"Then one day, she showed up with you in Baltimore. She told momma that you were her baby. Momma was always scared of Tammie so she didn't ask her any questions. Tammie told Momma that she needed her to keep you for a few days because she had to go back to New York to take care of some business. Then, she just left. That's all I know, Bolie," he said, sadly.

All I could do was start to crying. Uncle Horace tried to console me, but I wouldn't let him. I was mad as hell and just wanted to get off of the phone. I thanked him as best as I could and then hung up the phone. I just could not get my mind off of what he said about my name. It seemed to me that between him and Tammie it was just pulled out of some hat and used to label me. When I learned where the name came from it was very destroying and I no longer wasnted ownership of the name.

I felt a knot in my stomach. I was teased my entire life because my name was Symbolie. It was not the name to have. Other children had names like Michael, Donna, Jane, Lisa...you know, common names. Those names really meant something. My name means nothing, literally. I took the time to research my name and found nothing. I probably would have been able to ignore the taunting if someone had just taken the time to tell me that my name means this or my name means that. I know I would have held my head up high because it would have had significance.

I made up my mind right then and there to never ask Tammie for my papers again. I had to map this plan out for myself and work hard to get the answers I sought. I decided to start by using the business plan skill set that I had recently acquired to develop a master plan. I outlined all the steps I would take, including traveling to New York, and began gathering documents. I pulled all of the rejection letters out of the file and placed calls to the New York Department of Vital Records, Health and Human Services, and Social Security to acquire whatever documents I could. Once I had enough "evidence", I combed through each line by line and made notes along the way. I calculated the span of dates, used 1970 at my starting point, and put just enough of the pieces together to make my first trip to New York.

My first stop when I arrived was the police department. The intake officer informed me of the difficulty involved because events up to 1970 were not microfilmed. If there were any documents at all they could be found in storage in the basement...somewhere. To make matters worse, the officer shared the transitions taking place within the bureau over the years. Employees come and go and if accurate records were not kept there was really no telling what we would find if we went to the basement.

I was willing to take the chance and pick apart every file if necessary. Unfortunately, I was not granted access. I would need an order from the court to even have access to that area of the precinct. In spite of that, the officer was willing to look at the pictures and papers I had accumulated and offer whatever guidance he could.

I AM THE ANCESTOR

The officer led me to a room in the back of the precinct. It had one of those double glass windows that looked like a mirror from the inside but could be seen through on the outside. As I pulled out the papers, I shared bits and pieces of my childhood and how I suspected Tammie was not my mother. I shared the rape, the beatings, and the running away. I talked about the comments certain family members made over the years and how I began to feel like the ugly duckling. I told him that I needed answers not only for me but for the future of my children because they needed to know who their mother really was...and so did I.

I cried in between each word.

That intake officer sat there with tears welling up in his eyes. Motionless and speechless, he looked at the papers and the pictures and shook his head.

"How could somebody do that to a child?" he asked. "Miss Smith," he continued, "the only thing I remember was that there was an abducted kid in 1968."

My heart dropped and my eyes began to water. *Could it be me?*

Then he said, "That case involved a little boy. I'm very sorry, Ma'am."

I slowly gathered my documents and photos and place them back in the file. I thanked the officer for all of this help and then left the precinct.

My next stop was the library and hoped for better results there. I went straight to the Information Desk and requested the assistance of the librarian. I asked to see all newspaper articles form 1966, 1967, and 1968 involving missing children and abducted children. She then took me to the microfilm room, gave me a brief tutorial, and then I got started. Over the next three days for close to six hours each day, I looked at pages upon pages of articles and pictures of missing children to no avail. I felt defeated and decided that, for now, I would return home.

The drive back home seemed to take forever. I replayed the day's events over and over in my mind. Interrupting my thoughts along the way were the faces of those children I saw in the newspapers at the library. I wondered if they were dead or alive and, if alive, if they were pursuing answers to help form their correct identity. I then began to get angry with Tammie all over again: how could she be so cold and unfeeling to not give me answers?

I returned home from my trip and found piles of mail in response to the letters I sent to various agencies before I left for New York. Every single correspondence read "REJEC-TION", "Nothing on file to match request", or "Sorry, we cannot help you at this time." It had gotten so bad, the Department of Vital Records sent me a certified letter stating they had searched records from several bureaus using all possible names over the course of five years beginning with 1965 without a match at all. They then politely told me my case was closed and will not be reopened. In short, they told me to please not come back.

With rejection from Tammie and now the state of New York, I planned one final attempt to get answers. Using the little financial resources I had left, I printed 1,000 flyers that said, "Can you identify ME?", loaded them in my car and went back to New York.

Can you indentify ME...please?

CAN YOU IDENTIFY ME?

1968 or 1969   **1996**

SYMBOLIE MONIQUE SMITH

**Possible Abduction: 1968 or 1969
3rd Avenue & 174th Street - Bronx
Current Age 29 or 30**

Biological Mother's Possible Name: Margaret or Martha

I was one of six or seven children

I have an older sister with a large scar on the side of her face
(possible burn or birthmark)

PLEASE HELP ME FIND ME!

Call
Symbolie Monique Smith (collect calls welcome)
Phone or Fax (410) 435-2857

ELEVEN

Shut it Down and Look to the Children

WHEN I GOT BACK TO NEW YORK, I RANDOMLY selected a motel not too far from the library. I wanted to visit the spur of the moment if I found it necessary to do any additional research. With my highlighted map in hand, I found a corner to stand on for an entire day as if I were homeless and begging for spare change. Instead of receiving from people passing by, I wanted to give to anyone with an outstretched hand one of my flyers. I was certain that the information would pique their interest and give them a desire to help me find myself.

I imagined people stopping where I was and taking a flyer. I imagined that some of those same people would even entertain the details of my life story. I pictured them being very sentimental and compassionate towards me and willing to take a few extra flyers and share them with people they knew. I imagined that help would come, I would find my biological mother, and our sweet reunion would put a happy ending on my sad life.

Unfortunately, my imagination created nothing but a fantasy. Those flyers weren't leaving my hands quickly enough. I stood there for hours waiting for my happy ending but ended up heartbroken by the unresponsiveness of the people on the street. By the end of that first day, I had 973 flyers left. I was exhausted physically and mentally and ready to give up. It would have been just fine with me to toss those remaining flyers in the trash.

I began walking back to my motel room to turn in for the evening. It was the end of the workday and the nine to five workers were making their way back home. As I continued to walk, a gentleman stopped and introduced himself to me. I remembered him taking a flyer from me earlier in the day because he wore a bright red bowtie. Earlier, he was rushing to get to work. Now, he was walking at a slower pace.

"Hello. My name is Marc Rothberg. I work with a local newspaper not too far from here and was really interested in talking to you more about the flyer you gave me earlier," he said.

Totally shocked, I replied, "Oh my gosh! OK!"

We turned back around and began walking to Mr. Rothberg's office. I was exhausted and my feet were throbbing, but I got a burst of energy as a result of meeting him. I felt that this could be the big break I needed. Maybe...just maybe…someone would read my interview and claim me! When we arrived at his office, he offered me a beverage, and then took me to the conference room.

"Ms. Smith, your flyer caught my eye. I do believe you're the first missing person I've met who is actually reporting herself as missing. I'm fascinated to know what this is all about," he said.

I felt my emotions swelling up inside.

"How much do you want to know?" I asked.

"As much as you want to tell," he replied.

With that, I began talking.

I began to cry right away as I poured out the details of my life verbatim. Mr. Rothberg gave me a box of tissues and encouraged me to just continue talking as best as I could. I went back as far as I could remember and shared the very ugly details of how Tammie was a mother in name only. I cursed where I needed to curse to illustrate the way she talked to me and gestured to illustrate the blow of her fist. I told Mr. Rothberg how my uncles took turns stealing my innocence with no remorse and how one of those uncle's lives was snuffed out at a young age.

"In my opinion, he got what he deserved ," I said with no remorse.

He wrote down and recorded my every word. Intrigued by

our conversation and a bit in awe, Mr. Rothberg committed to a full write up which included my contact information. He promised to run it in the paper the next day. He gave me his business card and told me to keep in touch with him. He said should anyone call him with information, he would definitely contact me.

Once the interview concluded, we cordially parted ways and I went back to my room. All I could think about were my plans for the next day, which included calling a gentleman named Howard Terri, going through the archives at a New York City research center, and sleep. As soon as I showered and ate, I went straight to bed. It had been a very long day and it would be only a few hours before it all began again.

Bright and early the next morning, I took a cab to the research center and combed through papers dating back to 1968 and 1969. I read articles reporting any information on missing, stolen, or abandoned children. Most of the cases concluded with the children returned in body bags. There were a few stories where the children were returned unharmed which was always good to read, but it was very few.

Around noon, an old man sat at the table with me. I greeted him and he greeted me back. Then, he stuck out his hand as if to shake mine and told me his name was Dr. Tim White, a History professor at the City College of New York. Dr. White was there to research one of the wars that took place in America for an upcoming exam he was giving his students.

I AM THE ANCESTOR

When he saw all of my papers spread out on the table, he curiously began asking questions.

I told Dr. White just about everything I told Mr. Rothberg. Stranger or not, I knew the more I got my story out there the more people would know and begin to spread the word. Dr. White was blown away by what I shared. Before I knew it, he had stopped his research on the war and started helping me with mine.

We spent about three hours together going through microfilm. Slide after slide we jotted down any little piece of information that I could use to help me make sense of my life. He gave me great ideas on how to research and suggested that I use index cards in addition to using my notebook. Both were really good to write my notes on, but with index cards they were small enough to fit in the small pocket of my purse.

Before we knew it, Dr. White and I had spent a total of five and a half hours together working on my research. The center was about to close, so we had to wrap it up for the day. I did not quite know what to say to Dr. White. I never met this man before in my life, but he took time to help me piece my life together. I was extremely grateful to him.

Dr. White wished me well and told me that he would keep his eyes and ears out for anything he felt could help me. I gave him my address just in case he found something. He extended his hand to shake mine, but I gave him a big hug in stead. That encounter changed my life forever. Then, we left the center and I headed back to the hotel.

I had just one more thing to do and that was to call Mr. Howard Terri. Mr. Terri was a man Tammie knew in a very serious way. I believe they even dated for a period of time because his name was on a few pieces of government issued documents Tammie used to get certain services for me. About a month or so prior, I paid a company called Find People Fast a nice fee for a list of all of the Howard Terri names. They gave me every Howard Terri who lived across the county. In the part of New York Kim lived in at the time, there were over 1,000 Howard Terri's on the list. I checked off every "Howard Terri" that lived close to where Tammie lived and then I started calling.

In order for me to find the right person, I had to explain who I was and why I was calling. I always began by asking to speak to a Howard Terri who lived in the Bronx area of New York between 1967 and 1969. If he wasn't there, I would not leave a message. I would just let the person know I'd call him back later. If he was there, I went straight into who I was and the reason for my call. Once that was clear, I would ask if they had any information that would help me to find out who I was really was and where Tammie got me from.

I was somewhat concerned about how I would be received on the other end of the phone. When I really thought about what I was saying, I felt that some people would think I was some sort of crazy person on a mission to do them harm.

I AM THE ANCESTOR

This is why I was not surprised by the few people who just hung up on me. There were even some who threatened to have the call traced and then call the police. But, the more I thought about how close I was getting to answers, none of that mattered. I just kept calling and telling my story in hopes of getting more very important information.

The first several calls I made were not to the right Howard Terri. It was getting late and my eyes were starting to shut. It had been a very long day once again and all I really wanted was to go to bed. A couple of times, I took a break in between calls and lie back on the bed to rest a bit. Once I got a little more energy, I would move on to the next name on the list.

When I got to the next Howard Terri, the line was busy. I actually had the operator break through and a woman accepted the call. I was very surprised. Nevertheless, I began telling her my situation.

"My name is Symbolie Monique Smith and I am trying to find anyone who can help me piece my life together. My mother's name is Tammie Smith and..." I started.

"Tammie Smith?" the woman on the other end of the phone asked sort of surprised.

"Yes. Well, she's not really my mother but the woman who raised me. I believe she actually took me from a woman named Mary or Martha who lived in New York back around 1968 or 1969. I could not have been more than two or three at the time. I don't know exactly, but based on what other people have told me that seems to be the age. Over the past several months, I gotten lots of information from different people I have interviewed and collected many documents that I'm sorting through. I have a few papers in my hand with the name Howard Terri on it and I really would like to speak to him to see what he knows. I'm desperate for answers, Ma'am," I said without shame.

There was a very long pause. I did not know what to think or what more to say so I just sat there and waited. For a minute, I thought the woman hung up the phone but then I heard her sniffling. After that, she started crying. Thinking she was moved by my story, I tried to console her.

"Ma'am, I didn't mean to make you cry," I said.

Then, she said, "Howard Terri is my husband. We have been married for over 35 years. I know Tammie Smith and I know all about them and you. She ain't nothing but a house breaker, thief, liar, and whore. She tried to tear my family apart but it didn't work. Don't you ever call here again or I will call the police," she said. Then, she hung up the phone.

My heart jumped to my throat. This woman had the answers that I needed! I picked the phone back up again and called her right away. The phone just rang and rang. I hung up and called right back. The phone rang some more. When I hung up and called back a third time, the phone rang busy. So, I called the operator to have the call interrupted again. The operator told me that no one was on the phone. Instead, the phone had been taken off of the hook. I continued to call a little while longer and the phone kept ringing busy so I gave up trying.

I tried to piece together what just happened the best way I could. It seemed to me that Tammie and Howard Terri had an affair with each other over 30 years ago. He was married at the time while playing house with me and Tammie. Or, Tammie could have just been using him for money and using his name on certain documents in order get whatever she wanted. Either way, his wife found out at some point and Tammie and Mr. Terri stopped seeing each other.

At that point, I was too exhausted to think anymore. It was close to 10:00PM. Between crying until my eyes were bloodshot and my mind spinning around, the only thing I could do was go to sleep.

I woke up the next day still thinking about the call from the night before. However, I had to put that aside for the moment because I still had so much work to do and so much more ground to cover. The action plan was to pass out all of the 973 flyers at a different location. This time, I was a little more successful and distributed around 475 flyers. I became more comfortable and maybe even desperate to a certain degree. Whatever the case may have been, I was determined to get these flyers into the hands of people. I only had enough money to pay for two nights in the motel and two days of childcare. Using the little bit I had left over to eat, my money was starting to run very low. I had no choice but to make good use of the time I had left.

I began aggressively speaking to people and talking to them on the street. I asked questions about the changes in municipalities and whether or not there were changes in various bureaus. Surprisingly I learned more than I expected. Although I continued to encounter people who were cold and passed me by, I started feeling much better about what I had gotten done. Also, I felt relieved that I had made much more progress than the day before. I finally felt that I was not wasting my time.

When I got back to my motel that evening, I sifted through all my paperwork. As I zeroed in on one of the addresses Tammie used when she lived in New York, I remembered that she had a very close friend named Ms. Mable Spence who lived not too far away from us. When we moved to Baltimore, Tammie would visit her from time to time and took me with her now and again. They appeared to have a very close relationship.

It dawned on me that maybe Ms. Spence could help me get the answers I needed. I got really excited! This was as close as I could get at the time and I was going to go for it. I began to search for her in the white pages. With a name as common as hers, I made eight calls before finding the right Mable Spence. Once she realized I was "Tammie's girl" she immediately invited over to visit her while I was town. I told her I would be over the next day. I did not mention why

I AM THE ANCESTOR

I was in New York. I just told her that I had to take care of some business and that I would be returning back to Baltimore soon.

The following morning, I checked out of the hotel early and caught the subway to Ms. Spence's home. When I got there, she gave me a big hug and a kiss. She was still that sweet lady I remembered. She led me straight to the kitchen and told me to make myself comfortable at the table. There were chips and pretzels in a bowl and a few canned sodas out, too. She offered me a bite to eat, but I declined. I couldn't think about eating at the time. My mind kept twirling around at the thought of how close I was to getting answers.

"Oh, look how you have grown. I haven't seen you in so long," she said with another hug and a smile.

"Thank you, Ms. Spence," I said.

"I haven't spoken to your mother in years! How is she doing?" she asked

"OK," I struggled to say.

"That's good, Sweetie. Please, sit down and eat something," she offered.

We sat down and made small talk for a while about how things were going for her in New York and for me in Baltimore. I told her about Courtney and Christopher and showed her a few pictures. The time was passing by and I needed a way to get my thoughts out of my head and put them in our conversation. Just then, a way was made.

"What precious children you got there, Baby," she said, tenderly.

Seizing the moment, I said, "Ms. Spence, they are the reason I am here."

"What do you mean, Sugar?" she asked.

"Well, I'm trying to build a better life for all of us, but I keep getting stopped along the way because my papers are not straight. It's come to my attention that my mother is not sharing something with me. I've asked her repeatedly for my birth certificate and she cannot seem to produce one," I said.

Ms. Spence looked at me curiously but did not speak. I then told her more and more about the paperwork, the denials and the rejections, and my quest to get answers. Tears started to form in my eyes. The more I talked about my children, the more I missed them. I even started getting sad. This made me doubt myself and question why I was in New York in the first place. I started feeling the time I spent at Ms. Spence's house was a big mistake. If I could have rewind the day, I would not have gone at all.

The more I sat there, the more I cried, and the more I felt out of place. Ms. Spence patted my hand and told me that everything was going to be alright. It seemed a simple enough thing to do. It's funny how Tammie could never bring herself to share love that way. She had no feelings at all.

Just then, I made up my mind that I was just going to leave but Ms. Spence began to speak.

"Symbolie, I remember the first time that you came to my home with Tammie. She said she had just come from the store with you and immediately came to visit me. I said, 'Oooh, who is this little angel?' Then, Tammie told me that a woman she knew who hung out at the bar where she worked wanted her to watch you over the weekend. She told me that the children had other children who were with her at the time, but only asked her to keep you. She said the other children were about six, seven, and eight years old. Of course, I didn't think anything of it, just told her I was here to help. After that, she left and went back to her apartment. On Monday, Tammie came over again looking real mad and she said, 'Do you believe that she didn't come and get this girl?' I was shocked and asked her why your mother didn't come get you and she said she did not know," she said.

My stomach dropped as I thought about my mother possibly abandoning me. I tried to keep myself together, but began to cry very hard, Ms. Spence hugged me.

"You want me to stop, Baby?" Ms. Spence asked. Her concern for me was growing more and more.

"No! Please tell me more. I need answers, Ms. Spence. I'll be fine," I said, crying.

Ms. Spence continued.

"I remember that there were no clothes for you beyond a week so we went shopping. You would have thought that you were both of our baby. We got you clothes, toys, food... everything. You know women and babies! A few days passed and Tammie stopped by again. This time she was real angry and said that she was going to find your mother. She said she went knocking on doors where your mother hung out but no one would answer the door. I even asked if she was sure she was knocking on the right doors and she swore she was. I never bothered to suggest that I go with her. I just believed Tammie and took her at her word," she said.

I was in shock as I sat there listening to Ms. Spence. The more she talked the more I pictured everything she was saying. I remained as calm as I could but on the inside my heart was beating fast.

"We returned home that day," Ms. Spence said. "After a week of Tammie keeping you she told me that she never saw your mother at the bar again. She also said that every time she went back to the places where she hung out, people would tell her that they had not seen her. She decided to stop trying and asked if I would help by watching you while she was at work. We worked out a schedule because I had to work, too. Well, time passed and we just went on with our lives. Then, one day we were walking down the street and Tammie hunched me and said, 'Look at her. She doesn't even recognize her own daughter.' She pointed at a woman walking across the street and I thought it was your birth mother based on what Tammie said. I don't ever remember seeing that woman again, Symbolie," she said as her voice dropped.

"Did she ever say what my real mother's name was? If she couldn't find my real mother then why didn't she just call the police? I thought they were friends," I said, confused.

What Ms. Spence said next almost knocked me off of my feet.

"After two weeks of having you, Tammie wanted to keep you. That's why she didn't go on the other side of the street and approach the woman she claimed was your mother," she said.

"What do you mean 'she wanted to keep me'? That was against the law, Ms. Spence! She was supposed to take me to the police and tell them what happened. She was supposed to make sure that I got back to my real mother, not keep me like I was some little doll she found," I said in a very angry way.

I pulled out my papers and pointed to one of the names I'd seen on a few school records Tammie had kept.

"Who is this, Ms. Spence? Who is Daniel Banner?" I asked.

Ms. Spence shook her head.

"He's a man your mother used to live with when you were

very young. I think you were about four years old then. She met him one day at the bar where she worked. Sometimes we all hung out there when Tammie was off. Not more than two weeks later they started living together. Tammie always moved fast when it came to men. She felt that only the good ones stayed if you gave them what they want. Well, Daniel and your mother never got along. They argued all the time. When she felt he was going to leave her, she lied and told him that she was pregnant with twins. She carried that lie for as long as she could, but when he found out she was not going to have any babies, he was hot. He came real close to killing her for that. Not long after that, he split," she said.

I heard all I could stand for one visit. My mind was spinning and I started getting a headache. It was hard for me to not imagine what she was saying. It all really sounded like something Tammie would do. She was a huge liar and very manipulative. She knew what to do and what to say to get her way in any situation. Whenever it looked like someone was not going to help her, she would pull out all of her tricks to make them feel guilty. In the end, she really got what she wanted.

As I was gathering my things, I told Ms. Spence how long I had been in New York and what I was able to learn up to that point. I told her that I was going to take a break from my research and head back home to Baltimore because I really missed my children. I got all of my papers and put them back in the folder and then put the folder in my suitcase. Then, I thanked Ms. Spence for her time. We exchanged information and promised to keep in touch.

I went straight from Ms. Spence's house back to the hotel to the bus station. I was anxious to get back to Baltimore to see my children and wanted nothing more than to be with them.

During the trip home, I recapped all of the statements from everyone I'd interviewed. I thought about the time I spent in the library and at the archives and how my Creator sent a few strangers my way to help me along. I thought about all the flyers I handed out and how some people said they would keep in touch. My mind was spinning very fast. It was just too much to think of, too much to figure out, and too many pieces to the puzzle. In spite of all that, I had a million thoughts going through my head that just had to jot down in my notebook. Most of it did not make much sense to me, but I knew that in order for me to have even a little peace about all I heard, I had to get it on paper:

- ► The day Ms. Spence and Mommy were walking down the street and Mommy saw the woman she claimed was my biological mother, why didn't Ms. Spence say something? I don't think I would ever let a mother walk past her child and pretend not to recognize the child.
- ► Ms. Spence strongly believed Mommy's every word.

Why? What made Mommy so convincing?

- It is obvious that Mommy used Ms. Spence to get her help with clothes and food for me.

- If Mommy came home with me from someplace, then it's obvious I was never really dropped off. And if she told Ms. Spence that she was keeping me for the weekend, what made Ms. Spence think that the mother was "coming back" to pick child up from Mommy? When you tell someone you're "coming back" that means you had been there before. That's not what Ms. Spence said, unless she is just confused. Mommy came home with me. I was never dropped off so no one was "coming back."

- When Ms. Spence and Mommy went to search, in the beginning Ms. Spence said Mommy worked at the bar and my biological mother was a regular." If my biological mother never came back to get me from Mommy, then someone at bar would know something about her. They would have been able to help somehow. This is why I think Mommy brainwashed Spence.

- Ms. Spence sounded a bit confused. But she also felt real strong about what she was saying Mommy did, when she did it, how she did it.

- Mommy did not make any effort to give me back. She knew where my biological mother lived, what the other children looked like, the bar she hung out at, etc.

- Mommy fed Ms Spence's head with nothing but lies
- Mommy "decided she just wanted to keep me." What in the world was she thinking? You can't just "decide" to keep somebody. I'm a human being, not a toy.
- Ms. Spence said that all of a sudden I was gone. Mommy told her that she had found my biological mother and had given me back to her. I believe the same weekend she dropped me off in Baltimore with my grandparents she went back to NY and told Spence she gave me back.
- None of these stories match up.
- All these years, I believed Mommy saying she gave birth to me. For years she made me feel bad by saying I messed her up and caused her to not have more children. She lied and said my leg came out first then the doctor pushed me back inside. Then, the other leg came out and then my arm. All of that was pushed back in and then my head and neck finally came out. Strange how she never mentioned a hospital, boyfriend or nothing like that. She's liar all around.
- I do not believe she'll ever tell me the truth.
- First called the 42nd Street Manhattan precinct.
- The 42nd precinct said all records before 1970 was destroyed in a fire. Officer was nice enough to take me to the site of addresses where Mommy could have lived. But because many of the buildings were

old, the tore them down. Now they were just vacant lots.

- ▶ When I went to police department, learned that most of what I needed was archived.
- ▶ I worked through the state central registry and looked for information on myself.
- ▶ Learned that there were 241,425 persons born in 1966. Took me six hours to review 8,920 names. Never got a chance to go through all of them, so I just started jumping around between the year 1966 and 1969.

The trip, the search, the interviews, and the rejections cost more money than I planned to spend. Now, all of that money was gone.

I was very happy to see my children. I could tell that they really missed me because they would not let me go. *What a wonderful feeling it is to be loved.* I grabbed them and hugged them and kissed them a lot! My dear friend Paula took good care of them while I was away. Even though it was hard to leave them, knowing they were with her made it a little easier to go to New York.

My life picked up where it left off, but I just could not take my mind off of what I recently discovered. So, I jumped right into phase two of my action plan. I compiled a huge mailing list of celebrity talk show hosts, adoption agencies, missing persons agencies, state's attorney's, investigation bureaus, birth parent support networks, and main clearing houses which housed huge reference publications and materials. I was spending more money again. This time it was going towards paper, printing, stamps, and envelopes. Daily, I mailed each of them letters...sometimes as many as 20 a week.

Months passed before I received a reply. When many of the agencies did reply, they stated they could not help me. One agency said they "appreciated" me sharing the details of my life but they only provided help for people that were in adoptive or orphanage situations. They said if I did not have a social security number they would be able to at least run a search. Another one wished me luck and still another said they could not find any information on me and that there was nothing further to investigate. In short, I should just leave them all alone and let it go.

There were plenty of agencies that did not reply at all. No one could help me. Even the producers of Unsolved Mysteries told me that because my situation did not involve a cold case, they were not able to air the information. In short, if Tammie were dead they would have been able to help me. As much pain as I felt from what she did, I never wished her to be dead. I just wished she would give me answers.

Months of investigating where life began for me caused me to really lose focus. On top of that, I became extremely confused about practically everything. I did not know who I was or where I came from. The woman I knew all my life was not my mother after all. In fact, she purposely kept me from ever getting back to my real mother. My uncles were not my uncles and my grandparents were not my grandparents. I honestly felt like an alien who was disconnected from everybody except my children.

I decided to stop the mass mailings. It was no longer affordable. All my money was gone and I was consumed with all the typing and tracking of response. Along the way I began to realize just how much I was losing valuable time with my children. They deserved all of me. It was time to stop shortchanging them so, this time I was determined to let it go.

For the sake of my sanity and the welfare of Courtney and Christopher, I had to shut it all down, look to them, and resume my life as their mother. On top of that, fulltime work, recreational and educational activities for them, and a little time for me filled my plate. Slowly but surely, life became normal once more. I left my past in the past and decided that my present life was more important. I accepted that things were the way they were and moved on.

It took a while, but eventually I was able to let go of the need to search for answers. I was enjoying my children and all the time we spent together. Now and again, I would receive a small volume of mail from people who I met while on my journey in New York. A few of the people who worked at the library and the research center promised that they would look out for any information they felt could help me. They sent me just about anything and everything if they felt it would be a piece of my puzzle. Interestingly, I even had a couple of pen pals send a letter or two four months later. Apparently, they were passerby's on the street who took one of my flyers.

I received a bit of sad news in the mail one day as well. Carolyn White, the oldest daughter of Dr. White, wrote to share that her father has passed away rather suddenly. To my surprise, he took on my project as his own and continued to visit the research center in hopes of finding more missing pieces of my puzzle. Not only did Carolyn tell me of his death, she also sent me the file he created with all the details about me, and my life. It had everything that I shared with him, all information that we researched together, and additional information that I knew nothing about. When I realized that Dr. White continued to help me long after I left, I really felt honored and deeply touched.

In her letter, Carolyn stated that giving me the file was what her father would have wanted. She also said that Dr. White told her of all the information he researched in the years he was a professor, nothing was as fascinating as the story of my life. Carolyn wrote that her father spoke of me "with pride" and our chance meeting at the research center; he always said a prayer for me that I would find my real family.

TWELVE

My Only Gift...My Mini Empire

A REAL HARD LOOK AT MY LIFE REVEALED SOMETHING quite startling: I did not have an inheritance to leave my children. What a waste my life would have been to have them loose me and end up in the foster care system, or worse, left to raise themselves. That terrifying thought forced me to take a hard look at myself. When I did, I realized I was living from one week to the next and had nothing in the bank to fall back on. I practically exhausted every ounce of my savings as a result of going back and forth to New York. In essence, looking at myself helped me realize that I needed more to offer them. Because no one was going to die and leave an inheritance for me to pass onto them, I had to prepare for their future now.

Beautiful homes, trust funds, or priceless art were never lined up for me. Nothing! Everything I acquired was through my Creator's blessings all my life and lots of hard work over the past several years. It would have been great to come from a family that established my financial future. It would have been great to come from a family with a string of businesses, one waiting just for me to be old enough to run. It even would have been great to have someone hold me by the hand and guide me through the many processes of life I experience.

Unfortunately, that is not my story. You see, I come from a "family" that never lived, only survived. I come from a "family" who leeched off of each other to the point of resentment. My family would pay rent long enough to keep the Sherriff from knocking on the door and evicting them. They were the type to run three or four connected extension cords to the neighbor's house when the electricity got cut off. They were scam artists who took advantage of any and everybody just to get what they want. They were pimps and hustlers in their own right when all they had to do was work hard like the majority.

My "family" drove cars without licenses and stole stickers off of car tags to place on their own. Purchasing car insurance never occurred to them. If they got in an accident they would not stop to see what was damaged. They would just keep driving. They would climb the BGE poles and replace the fuse with a penny so the meter would misread and the cost of the electricity would be lowered. And, when BGE finally caught up with them, they would run a kerosene heater for months at a time before the paid that bill.

I was raised by a group of uncivilized human beings, a pack of wolves who stopped at nothing to cut corners illegally. I will never forget the time when Tammie got really, really sick. Unlike times past, she could not just take come cough syrup and rub her body down with alcohol and the problem would go away. She really had to go to the doctors. So, she decided to use her cousin's name, insurance card, and even parts of her medical history to get treatment.

No one was except from being part of a scam...not even me. To this very day, my front top tooth reminds me of a scam gone wrong. Uncle Roger was in the mood for breaking into an abandoned house. He took me along with him to help. I was either 11 or 12 years old. When we found the house he wanted, he helped me climb through the window and told me to open the door for him. When I let him in the house we went straight to the basement. Uncle Roger wanted the water heater. As we were loosening the screws, it fell back hitting me in my mouth and chipping my top tooth. The pain was so severe I screamed. Uncle Roger grabbed me and we got out of the house. Guess when I got my tooth fixed? When I was an adult who was old enough to pay for it herself.

There was another time when we were driving down the street and we passed a furniture store. Uncle Roger said, "Hmm. I'm going to get my furniture one day." Even thought he did not act on that comment, I knew that if he wanted it badly enough, he would do whatever he could to steal it.

I AM THE ANCESTOR

I come from a fighting "family", too, who never backed down from anyone or anything. They not only fought each other, but literally tried to kill each other. If any of them were wronged, offended, or even looked at sideways, the poor person who did either or all of those things were really going to get it good. No one was excluded so it did not matter if you were young or old. I'm sure that does not come as a surprise after reading how Tammie beat me all of my life.

Once, Tammie and Uncle Horace were having a heated argument. It was really my first time seeing my uncle act this way. Usually when he and Tammie were at it, he would usually have a few words with her and then simply walk away. He never wasted his time going back and forth with Tammie because he knew she lived to argue. Anyway, Tammie crossed the line and tried to swing at Uncle Horace. In not time flat, hr picked up Tammie and throw her down the stairs.

On another occasion, Tammie and Uncle Roger got into a fist fight that could have gone down in boxing history. She was throwing those blows at him like she was going for the championship title. Uncle Roger grabbed Tammie and just started pounding her on her arms and on her back. Eventually Tammie managed to get away from him. She ran straight into the kitchen and grabbed the rifle hanging behind the door. My grandmother was in the kitchen at the time this was happening. When she saw Tammie grab the gun, she started going after her. Well Tammie, who was not backing down, actually pulled the trigger just as my grand-mother jumped in the way. The gun backfired and snapped Tammie's hand causing it to get burned.

"You trying to kill somebody, bitch? I got something for your ass," Uncle Roger said. Then, he beat her in the face, grabbed her around the neck and started choking her, punched her in the stomach, and stomped her in the face. Tammie's ribs were cracked as a result and her eyes were swollen shut.

Another time, Uncle Roger and Uncle Horace were going at it. I don't recall of the details because I was on punishment and told to stay in my room. All I remember is hearing the sound of glass breaking. I ran out of my room and down the stairs into the living room. I saw my grandmother screaming and crying and lots of blood on the floor. When I got a lit-tle closer, I saw my grandmother outside with Uncle Roger. I could tell that he had been cut and that's when I realized that Uncle Horace threw him out of the large pane glass win-dow by the front door. Someone called the ambulance and the only thing Uncle Roger received were lots of bandages.

Although this is how my "family" chose to live, I chose dif-ferently. I am the first in my "family" to earn a high school diploma. I am the first in my "family" to own two houses and keep them. I am even the first in my "family" to work a job for more than a year and, of course, the first in my family to even think about becoming an entrepreneur. In their eyes, I'm sort of like The Kennedy's! All of my cousins have had run-ins with the law for one thing or another. Their crimes were major: larceny, attempted murder, fraud. Many of them have spent months and even years in prison. I know that, statically, I should have gotten caught up in "the game" and merely existed alongside of them. But, God obviously had a greater plan for me.

The choices I made to be the very best I could be helped me to focus on what mattered most with my children. It occurred to me if I didn't work towards giving them something, their lives would be meaningless and full of work by the sweat of their brow. Wasting no time, I went from thinking about preparing for my children's future to putting those thoughts into action. I worked more, saved more, and lived a real frugal life. I learned the art of shopping off-season to get the best prices and simply packed away the items until the season rolled around again.

Spending as little money as I could, I invested all extra monies into developing Courtney and Christopher. Swimming lessons, boy scouts, girl scouts, chess club, and every possible educational need was met. I made sure they participated in all of their school activities and field trips. On the weekends, we would hang out at the museums, the park, or drive to Washington, DC for various parades and festivals. My children were very well rounded and exposed to just about everything you can imagine.

Courtney and Christopher had the life I never had but always dreamt of having. They were typical children who focused on being children. They had a mother who loved, nurtured, and protected them by any means necessary. Their home environment was safe and lacked nothing. By virtue of my childhood experiences, I typically took them with me wherever I went because trusting others was very hard to do. The only time they stayed with someone for an extended period of time was when I went to New York. Even then, I checked on them throughout the day.

Serious concerns about my identity played out in my head often. Because I had no real documentation to prove who I was, I strategically planned to continue living under the radar. I often wondered what would happen to me if any-one found out I was not who I was. Worse, I wondered what would happen to my children. Would they be taken away from me? Would I be jailed or sent away someplace?

As a result, I stayed away from opportunities that would force me to produce my birth certificate, social security card, or other paperwork. I can not begin to tell you how much I missed out on because of this. For one, I was not able to travel anywhere outside of the United States or its proper-ties. The same is true today. What I would not do to set my feet on the sandy beaches of the Bahamas or Jamaica!

Furthering my education halted immediately. I did not attend college, take any certification classes, or participate in other programs because I was too afraid. The risk was too great and, although I had gotten by in the past, I was not willing to take any chances. Myself aside, I had to think about what was in the best interest of Courtney and Christopher. Instead, I taught myself at the library and practically everyone became my "E.F. Hutton." If someone spoke, I listened and absorbed the information if it was suited along the path I was travelling.

Fortunately, my plan worked for a couple of years. I moved along undetected and was able to build a substantial savings. I developed a life of discipline and stuck to my plan. I had a goal and I was not going to let anyone or anything hold me back. I was tempted at times to spend a little here and there for a "must have" item. But, I kept reminding myself that I was building this savings for my children's future.

Courtney, Christopher, and I lived a most fulfilled life. They truly brought me so much joy! When I felt it was time to invest my savings, I took the risk of purchasing a second home. It was truly a leap of faith for me. As fearful as I was, the transaction went very well. I was determined to leave something behind for my children. Now with two pieces of property, each child would be able to benefit should something happen to me.

In the meantime, Christopher, Sr. I maintained a very strong relationship for the betterment of the children. Most importantly, we had a solid friendship and supported each other professionally as well. As an entrepreneur trying to make his mark in Baltimore and beyond, I committed myself to help him in anyway I could. He was a far cry from the type of men that I grew up watching.

Christopher lived a very honest life and worked hard for everything he earned. He worked with his hands and rarely hired additional laborers to assist him. Although we are not presently in a relationship with one another, we communicate very well and are mutually focused on the needs of the children first. I have never married nor lived with him, however, our children know good of their father. I have never talked badly about him to them. I don't understand why women do that, by the way. It only hurts the children.

Even though the children have never gone with him or his side of the family for an extended period of time, they do know of them. This is just the way the relationship has always worked out. The children have asked a time or two before why we have never gotten married or lived together. My response to them is simple: that's the way our relationship has been and will continue to be.

As life would have it, Christopher and I had two more children together. We named the Xavier and Katlyn. They are a little more than three years apart. For me, it was a dream come true to become a mother once more. My desire was to have six children, but four was a great blessing!

Just as with Courtney and Christopher, Xavier and Katlyn were going to have the best that life could offer by any means necessary. All four of my children would want for nothing and learn the importance of looking out for each other. I would model for them why valuing every person they meet was not a matter of choice. It was a given, a must in order to have a peaceful life. They would excel in school and pass the knowledge on to anyone who had a desire to learn.

I pride myself in being a mother! There is no greater title that I would ever want to bear. I am not an aunt, a niece, a daughter nor a cousin. I am a mother! I am their number one fan who cheers for them at every game, every recital, and everything else with ease and much pleasure. I love them for life! I'm hoping that whatever motherly instincts I did not glean from Tammie instinctively lives inside of me.

I'm often asked, "Monique, what is your passion? What is your desire, your vision?" Without hesitation, I respond like this:

> *"I am in love with me! I'm in love with being a mom! That is my only passion! I'm not opening up a bakery, not getting my real estate license, no quest to tour the world, no emptiness to acquire an Associate, Bachelors, or Masters Degree. I will just forever want to nurture my children and thank him for I am able!"*

THIRTEEN

I Am Free and My Children are More Empowered

S**UFFERING THE ABUSE IN TAMMIE'S HOUSEHOLD AND** under her watch left me to wrestle with a major lack of love. I never heard her say "I love you, Bolie" and I only used those three words towards her as a means of protection. There were no hugs, encouragement, support, or guidance...not even when I was in the hospital for months recovering from deadly syphilis. There was no one to look up to as a role model and no one could ever really share who I was as a person, a sweet little girl, a normal child.

The people I have mentioned throughout this book looked through me as if I never existed. Although they were present, they were not aware of my day-to-day life struggles and the obvious disconnection between Tammie and me. They never questioned why there was never any "mommy-time" or one-on-one cuddling with Tammie while reading a bedtime story. And they cared less that my bedtime prayer was not "Now I lay me down to sleep...", but simply "God, help me!"

I have missed out on much of what others take for granted. For example, being able to share stories with my children like, "Your great-great-great-grandfather was the first chauffeur for the White House" or "Baby, your hair is nice like that because we have a bit of Indian in us from your grandmother's side of the family." Hearing my oldest son say, "Dang, mom! We've never even been to a relative's house out of state," or my oldest daughter say, "Mom...I have to do annual testing on just about everything because of no family medical history" will forever serve as a reminder that my story really begins with me.

It is a blessing that my Creator made me the woman that I am today. I was spared from the possibilities of being lamed, mentally retarded, or even dead just so I could be the mother, aunt, and Godmother to my children in a way that would not scar them for life. I have been able to teach myself much of what I know and survive everything that I experienced while keeping a genuine smile on my face. I am able to leave, among other possessions, an extra house for my children as if I inherited it from my family. Statistically, this is unbelievable and would certainly cause many to say, "Wow!"

Coasting through life over the years with little or close to nothing is really a miracle! I know that I could have been another statistic and my remains could have been found in an abandoned house or dark alley. I know that my body could have been dumped in a stream and never found again. Instead, I have the ability to walk, bathe, talk, work, and breathe without the assistance of anyone or anything. Through it all, I have managed to keep it all together with every bit of power that my Creator gifted me so I can be of service to him, my children, and myself.

If I had to use one word to describe what has resulted from my life experiences, that word would be character! I have built some of the best and most amazing connections over the years. Many are the relationships and bonds I have established have ensured countless resources and over-whelming support. Often I'm told by many that my ability to see the best in everyone and aid them along life's journey is sincerely heartfelt. I have shared my home to allow a person in need to grow and develop, educated kids with a desire to instill in them teamwork, and have even used my name to provide services and authority where others could not.

I cringe each and every time I hear or see that an Amber Alert has sounded. I can hear the voice of a mother, father, or caregiver who is pleading to have their child brought back home safely or just back to their family. My heart grieves with every person who has to attend a candlelight vigil on the anniversary of the abduction, or murder of their loved one. I can see the image of that mother looking out into space for that missing loved one to appear and envisioning what life would be like if all of the plans they intended for them came true.

But then, I snap out of my daydream feeling a void and realize I am that missing child. Is there someone, anyone, somewhere still looking for me? Is a mother, sister, or aunt saying, "I know she is out there; she's alive...I just feel it." Maybe they have decided to leave a plate for me at the cookout or a note telling me that they are running to the store and will be right back. Perhaps someone remembers that little two year old girl and asks, "Whatever happened to her?"

I am the ancestor. Before I die, I must share my story for no one else can!

I am only sharing my story now for the sake of my children. It would be a disservice if any of them did an ancestry or genealogy search to find out that their own mother was not Symbolie Monique Smith. While I am not looking to make up for the 40 plus years of being missing and don't wish to hear things like, "Oh, Honey, I am so sorry but he/she died. If you had come about five or so years back, you would have seen your mother/father/sister/brother. My God, how you look just like them," I will embrace any linkage to my past. Meeting a relative after all these years to connect with them to play "catch-up" is always a possibility, but not a priority.

I refuse to just leave behind businesses, a life insurance policy, homes and other materials possessions without sharing with them my true identity and my life's journey. This will enable them to have a greater appreciation for the legacy and see it as foundation to build upon. Often I have shared with them the importance of representing yourself by your name. Something as simple as knowing your name, what it means, and from where you come is empowering! From the beginning of our existence, just hearing one's name brings strength in itself; it is a rewarding experience that requires nothing but your inner spirit and your determination to be proud of yourself. That is something no one can take away.

The joyous moments that I have with my children are the direct opposite of the horrific moments that I had with Tammie. I call them by name and I make sure they know I love them. I am there to cheer in my sports paraphernalia during my boy's practices and games. I am there with my flashy, handmade signs at my daughter's soccer games. I'm there to tuck my little girl in bed for the night, lie beside her until she falls off to sleep or both if that is what she desires. This is the essence of my freedom and I know it came at high price that I would pay all over again if it meant my children could have the life they live or greater!

I am free because no longer do I have to fake a family that never existed. I don't have to pretend that Uncle Samuel and Uncle Roger, who raped me against my will, were the type of uncles the average family would love to have. I can finally stop perpetrating a mother and daughter relationship with an individual who, at times on a subhuman level, never had any real purpose or pure intentions for me at all.

I AM THE ANCESTOR

I am free because while I had to live the way I did for survival and know my path was really on the road less traveled, I managed to keep alcohol out of my system and a needle out of my veins. Choosing to not expose my children to my horrific childhood, teenage life, young adulthood, and pre-mom lifestyle was how I kept them free from transferred baggage. I am free because I've discovered all along that I possess the most genuine gift of selflessness a person has ever known in spite of being robbed of everything from my body to my money.

I am free because after resolving to share my story, I removed the burden Courtney would have felt if left with the task of revealing my true existence to her younger siblings. Through these pages, I will fight the fight they will be unable to fight in the event of my death. I am free because I acknowledged the urgency to validate my existence for them and not leave it to a person who did not have all the facts.

I am free because if I died there is nothing left to ponder or wonder. No more guesswork; no more to add or take away. Courtney, Christopher, Xavier, and Katlyn do not have to fear the whispers from the rumor mill or worry about my association to a secret. It has all been exposed right here in this book. The burden that I carried for far too many years has now been lifted and this "dungeon kid" has finally surfaced. I am free!

My children are empowered because they will NOT have to

suffer like I did. They're enriched because knowing the true depths of which I had to survive to become the woman that I am today for them to know how many breaths that I had to fight to breath just for them to have breath.

Once I decided to stop searching for answers to my past and shifted all of my attention back to my children, my life blossomed in a way that removed a great deal of the pain. I began to form many positive relationships with people from all walks of life. As trust was built, I began to share with a few what I experienced as a child. Needless to say, the support and overall response was completely overwhelming! Even as I write this book, there are many people who do not know my story. However, both those who know and even those who do not know have equally aided me in my journey.

Here, I'd like to introduce you to just two of my friends who have been simply the best! Please, hear from them:

I met my best friend at work over 20 years ago. When we first met, we never thought we would become so close. Many are still amazed at how close our friendship has remained. One can say we are like peanut butter & jelly or salt & pepper, while we are very different, we are perfectly matched and that has made for such a beautiful friendship/sister hood. Most people select their friends by the amount of time they hang out with them. But a best friend, is someone you can rely on a 100%, it's a part of yourself. Best friends are created from your attitude; it's not a matter of the words but a matter of the actions and dedication you each display.

Mo and I have stayed friends because we have always been able to be honest with each other regardless if we knew that it was not what the other wanted to hear. We both understood that being a true friend meant being honest and that we would not always agree but we would always respect one another's decision and be there for each other.

Mo is painlessly honest and the most upbeat person I know. She will show up early for a party to help you set up or give you a small gift just because it reminded her of you. Mo doesn't gloat about her generosity and might not even realize how much her actions mean to people. However, to me, these are actions of a good person. But what I truly appreciated and come to love her for was the times when she's pointed out my flaws and pushed me to be more honest with myself.

She is beautiful and empathetic and reacts strongly when she feels an injustice has been committed (As you will learn from reading her book). I am at awe at her ability to run a demanding office, raise 4 children, be a mentor to young girls, and still make time for her friends. But I am most impressed with her ability to wear a smile and stay upbeat about life while housing the pain from her past and working so hard to learn of her true identity. In case I'm incorrectly making her sound overbearing or self-righteous, she's in fact delicate, creative, and full of life.

Mo is the kind of person you could call any time of day or night and she would be there to listen with both ears and always offer you a word of encouragement and a hand if you need one. By the end of the conversation, Mo would always have you convinced that everything was going to be okay

If I was asked to describe my friend I would have to say she is Funny, supportive, sensitive, cheerful, a straight (frank) talker and a person with a huge heart. Between us, it is a "receiving-giving" sisterhood that i am sure, will never end.

To me these quotes best identify our friendship

"True friendship isn't about being there when it's convenient; it's about being there when it's not."

"Best friends are the ones who can be the farthest away but there the fastest when you call."

"A true friend is someone who is there for you when he'd rather be anywhere else".

"A friend is someone who knows the song in your heart, and can sing it back to you when you have forgotten the words."

I just want to say Thanks and I love you for being like a sister to me. No matter how long it's been since we last talked or hung out you are always there to share the good and the bad. You make me laugh when i feel like crying and you make me move when i feel like doing nothing. I am in awe of the person you have turned out to be. You are someone any parent would be proud to have as a daughter. You are an amazing mother, friend and leader. But most of all you are my best friend but more like my sister.

— Rosalyn McKinney

****

Over the last fourteen years of my teaching career, I have yet to meet a more active and involved parent as Monique Smith. Monique's ability to touch the lives of everyone she meets is amazing. She utilizes the most important skill that teacher's find most effective in spurring student growth: modeling. Through her kindness, her compassion, and her enthusiasm for helping all of those around her, Monique demonstrates the power that one person can change the world around her. I don't know how she does it all with such exuberance and success. From working full-time, to establishing and guiding her own community outreach programs for the empowerment and betterment of women and children, to enthusiastic, hands-on parenting, to supporting teachers and students at rallies, to working on the P.T.A., to volunteering regularly for school functions, there is never a task from which Monique shies away. She has personally made my experience as a teacher much more rewarding in so many ways. I could call her (and still do!) with any need, and she would be right there to help in any and every way she could. Most importantly, Monique has taught me that there are people out there in the world with a kind heart and a farmer's "get down and dirty" work ethic, who will do whatever it takes to both support and contribute to the growth and well-being of our youth.

Monique seems to have made it her own personal mission to make the world a better place, starting with her own beautiful children. Well-rounded, intelligent, and full of wonder, her children are her legacy and will surely go on to spread the same kind of generosity and kindness throughout their community and the world. How could they not, after all? They are blessed with a mother who models and exemplifies the characteristics of a true teacher, one who looks beyond the kitchen table, beyond the front yard, beyond the books, beyond classroom walls. Monique looks within, utilizing the power of one's self, to lead and shape the lives around her.

— Kimberly Brause (Kimberly Heckel)

FOURTEEN

A Conversation with Jack and a Letter to Abductors

THE MOMENT I DECIDED TO WRITE THIS BOOK, I KNEW that I wanted to donate a portion of the proceeds to an organization that worked to help stop child abductions and rescues missing and exploited children. I decided to call a friend of mine named Jack who actually hosts an annual event to help raise funds for an organization called You are Never Alone or YANA for short.

The mission of YANA is to reach out in love to women and girls involved in prostitution, offering alternatives to those seeking change and compassionate support for women exploited by any aspect of the life. Their mission is accomplished through street outreach (daytime and evening/night); hospitality (food, clothing, showers, resources, offered in a homelike setting); trauma counseling/therapy; case management; advocacy; and diversion services (YANA HOPE). YANA's clients, staff and Board members also engage in advocacy work in the Baltimore area, statewide, and on a national level.[1]

****

"Hey, Jack! I'm writing a book about my life and I want to donate a portion of the proceeds to YANA because I'm one of them. How do I go about doing this?"

"Hey. Monique! Wow, a book? What are you not doing? That's awesome. You never told me that you were a member of YANA. I know you always come to the events, but I didn't know about your membership."

"Well, I'm not actually a member. I'm just one of them."

"What do you mean you're 'one of them'?"

"I mean I am a missing and exploited child who is now an adult. I've recently decided to write a book about my life and all of my experiences to bring awareness to the fact that some of us are still alive and living as normal a life as we can. We work like every day people, raise families like every day people, and like to have fun like every day people. The only difference between us and them is that we don't know who we are as a missing and exploited child and want to

---

1. "Organizations." Humantrafficking.org. http://www. humantrafficking.org/organizations/390. (19 August 2011)

help others like us. I feel the best way to do this is to support your organization. I've known all about the work you are doing and want to continue to support you on a more regular basis."

I began sobbing uncontrollably, but continued to speak.

"I think I was about one or maybe two when the woman I've known as my mother abducted me. Along the way, I began prostituting so I could survive. I'm not quite sure how Tammie, the woman who raised me acquired me because I've gotten different stories from different people. I began my search many years ago, but it became too time consuming. My life was totally interrupted from all of my traveling between Maryland and New York. I was gone for weeks at a time. At the time, Courtney and Christopher were small and I could tell they were beginning to understand that mommy was not around that much. Now that they are much older and my lack of identity is starting to affect their ability to do something as simple as travel to another part of the world, I am doing whatever I can to bring exposure to my situation."

"You know, it was fine when I came to terms with the fact that I will never be able to take a trip to the islands. And, it was fine when every single application to start a business in the state of Maryland got rejected one by one. It was even fine when I realized that I would never be able to go back to school to get a college degree even though I wanted to more than anything. But, it's not fine for anyone or anything to touch my children in anyway! This life that I've been forced to live is getting in the way of their progress and causing their dreams to be deferred. So, I've got to do something. I just can't sit here and let them suffer the way I did. It's not fair."

"Jack, I have the best children a mother could have ever prayed to have. You know that. They don't give me an ounce of trouble. They work hard at school and at home. They are very respectful, honest, full of love, and really care about other people. Now, don't get me wrong: they are typical children. But, when I say that they will give their last so another person won't be without, I mean just that! This is why I'm going back to the beginning to try to put all the pieces together as best as I can for all of us. I'm also going to tell my story to anyone who will listen because it's just that important to me."

"I know I'm not alone. I know that there are hundreds, maybe even thousands of people in the world just like me. We are blue collar workers and white collar workers. We are teachers, doctors, construction workers, and lawyers. We have gone on with our lives, gotten married, and had children knowing that we will never truly be complete. The 'short end of the stick' will be our motto forever because of the way we have been cheated out of our lives and the chance to grow up with our real families. We were not adopted legally but given away, snatched, and stolen. It's so unfair to wonder and wonder and wonder 'Where do I belong? Where do I fit in?'"

I AM THE ANCESTOR

"I can't begin to tell you how many times I've walked down the street looking into the faces of strangers and tried to figure out if they were possibly a cousin, a sister, or even my mother. Or, how many times I've driven down the beltway and saw an Amber Alert just to begin crying my eyeballs out while praying for that child to be returned to her or his family. It's so hard to listen to the news and learn that another little body has been found in the river. How in the world could someone do that to a child?"

"Two months ago when I heard not one, but two reports of adults who came forward to tell they had been abducted as a child, I was happy and sad all at the same time. Happy that they were finally going to get a chance to reunite with their biological family, but sad that they had lost so many years with that same biological family. Even though I'm not on a mission to find my biological family, I hope that by telling my story something great will come out of all of this! I just know it will."

Then, there was nothing but silence on the other end of the phone.

"Jack? Jack, are you there?"

I heard Jack take a deep breath.

"Monique, I'm so very sorry. I never knew that you were one of the faces of a missing and exploited child. I've known you for years and always thought you had a normal childhood and life like most people. I've never received a call like this in

all of the years I've been working here. Today, you have put a new face on what it means to be a missing and exploited child. I am hopeful that the work we do here will continue to help people like you...and put abductors out of business!"

"Thanks, Jack."

"Please keep me posted on all of your progress and when your book is released. I really want to buy a copy. I'm going to transfer you to Tina who will help you, Monique. I'll talk to you later."

In a matter of seconds, I was speaking with Tina. I briefly recapped the purpose of my call and asked how the organization could officially receive a portion of the proceeds from every book sold. I even asked what procedures I needed to follow if I wanted to host events in their honor. YANA had done great work in the Baltimore area for many years and I wanted to help them continue the great work they were doing.

When I got off the phone with Tina, I sat at my desk and thought about what just occurred. For nearly thirty minutes, I shared my story with two people who had instantly embraced me. They were determined to help me just as much as I was determined to help them. By the time we hung up the phone, all of our lives had been changed forever in a way none of us ever imagined.

****

I AM THE ANCESTOR

October 2, 2011

A Letter to Abductors:

For close to 25 years, I've waited for an opportunity to address you. Well, now my time has come and you're going to hear what I have to say!

Your wicked schemes and deadly abuse has transformed the lives of millions of people all across this world. It is quite clear that you do not pattern your life after the principles found in the Bible. If you had, soulless person, you would have clearly learned that kidnapping is forbidden and punishable by death. Considering you do not value your own life, I guess it's crazy of me to think you would ever have the heart to value another person's life.

What compels you to steal a child? I mean, how can you just walk away from a park, a schoolyard, a hospital, a playground, a mall, a grocery store, or even a home with someone's child...and keep on walking? What possesses you to knock a woman upside her head, leave her in an unconscious state, and kill her as you brutally remove the embryo from her womb as if it was normal behavior? What drives your deceitful, sickening, manipulative agenda that causes you to brainwash others who aid you unbeknownst to them? What in the world are you thinking? Are you thinking at all?

What is the real purpose for your unbelievable actions? When you look at our beautiful faces do you only see "tax deduction", "government assistance", or "ticket for a free meal?" Why, I ask you; do you merely being us out of hiding to suit your needs? Why do you think it is necessary to take this route to become a parent? You fool! Don't you realize that there are countless legitimate options for you? If you had birthed a child yourself, would you treat them the same way you treated us?

How can you be so void of feeling? How can you be so empty and emotionless to believe that it is acceptable to turn a blind eye every time an innocent life is physically, mentally, verbally, emotionally, spiritually, and sexually abused? Why the abuse at all? Do you like pain? Do you possess a spirit? Are you giving thought to any of my questions? If so, have you thought about what if it had been you?

Miss Abductor, it is important for you to know that I would have preferred to stay at that playground the day I was snatched. I enjoyed the see-saw, sliding board, and monkey bars. Sure, I probably would have gotten hit upside my head accidentally by a swing I left too soon. But I sure would have preferred the knock upside my head by that swing rather than being knocked around the bedroom by the intentional swing of a 2x4. I would have preferred to cry to the top of my lungs for something I couldn't get at the mall versus breaking the sound barrier for crying because there was no loving connection with you at all.

Look, you insane, incapable invalid, my quest to find my identity has revealed that I have unknowingly falsified my four children's birth certificates. Your thoughtless actions has made me out to be a liar! You see, because I was abducted, Symbolie Monique Smith is not my birth name. This name I have lived with for close to 45 years...I think... was forced upon me by a woman just as crazy as you are. She had absolutely no rights to me at all. No rights at all! Because of all this, the name under "Mother" on my children's birth certificate actually belongs to someone else or no one at all. That name you gave me means nothing.

I wish I could tell you what my real name is, but you never took me back so I could ask my real mother. You never gave me a chance to say "Goodbye", give her a final hug, or wave as I was led down the street. For all I know, it could be ...well, pick a name, any name!

You selecting me for your personal use never gave me an identity or a sense of self-worth. It is only through the help of my Creator that I have become the woman I am today.

The silver lining around this cloud of emptiness and extreme absence of truth is how blessed I have been to have a vision of motherhood since early on in my youth. For as long as I could remember, I desired to be the best mother that I could be! Although I lacked that example in my life, I knew that I would never treat a child the way I was treated. I knew that what was called "love" was not love at all. I knew way deep down inside of me that the type of pain I experienced was not normal by any stretch of the imagination. I kept hoping and praying that one day the pain and suffering would stop. Well, one day came and it's here today!

I now who and what I am! I am Symbolie Monique Smith transformed by the power of my Creator's love! I am a woman of all women who loves life with all of its ups and down. I am mom to four priceless children named Courtney, Christopher, Xavier, and Katlyn who are great and will continue to be great! I am defining M.O.M. as Monique's Own Manual and creating this customized system just for my children so I can give them their identity the best way I know how. I am all that and so much more!

One moment at a time, I have gained strength to share my story with merely a handful of people through the years. Those conversations never came easily for I cried with every other word and would often have to stop because the sobbing caused my words to become unrecognizable. Bitter feelings and unforgettable reactions would leave them swearing *that my survival is a miracle! They concluded, and I concur, that there have been others in my position would did not make it out alive or, at the very least, sane. Look here, you despicable animal, I was spared and this book is that reason why!*

My writing everything I've written has allowed my children to escape with me. In fact, I have found a way to set them free in more ways than one. They are free to know the truth and live the life I never had. They are free to go places I've never been and experience cultures I'll never know. They are free to know that you are out there and that you don't always look like the ugly and disfigured creature they have seen in the movie.

On the outside you look like an everyday person. You present yourself as the neighbor next door, the preacher in the pulpit, or the mailman who always ring twice. Your disguise resembles the football coach who runs down the sidelines to see the touchdown first hand, the department store cashier ready to be of service, or the bartender mixing drinks at the night club. Sadly, you even look like a loving mother, firm father, or gentle grandparents ready to kiss the boo-boo's and make everything feel better.

In reality, you're nothing but a lifeless, mentally retarded, shell of a human being whose card has been peeped. Society is so aware of your new attempts to capture, imprison, harm, or kill kids and adults, male and female alike. Organizations, technology, people all around the world are on alert and keeping their eyes out for you at an alarming rate.

How do I know? Well, I took my child into the emergency room not long ago for a very minor injury. Before I could take my seat, I was held accountable immediately to provide every bit of information about my child, myself, and the injury. Short of giving my blood type, I was asked one question after another in an attempt to prove to them I was who I said I was, my child was really my child, and the injury was the result of an honest accident.

These measures are in place to keep children safe at all cost. I know that there are still leaks in the system, but overall greater protection is being provided. Even though you think you have gotten away, you have not. It's only a matter of time before you are hung by your actions and punished for the crime. And, when that day comes, I'll be watching with pride that you are off the streets and another child is saved.

Meaning everything, I said,

—Monique Smith

FITHTEEN

Possible Role Player: YOU?

REFLECTING ON MY LIFE, I CAN SEE HOW THERE WERE family members and friends alike who just stood by and watched me suffer at the hands of Tammie and my uncles. I was kicked, slapped, punched, slammed, and pushed, shoved, slung, and nearly choked to death in the most obvious of ways. My innocence was taken at the age of four and my virginity was snatched away from me at the age of thirteen by a sick minded uncle while others were in the house at the time. To make matters worse, his brother thought it was fine to do the same. They raped me over and over again mentally as well as physically. They stole a piece of my very soul and had no intention on giving it back. Yet, my family did nothing to help me. Even Miss June saw first hand the bruises Tammie put on my body using a 2x4 piece of wood and all she did was put her hand over her mouth and shake her head.

I have my hand over my mouth and I'm shaking my head,

too. Except, I do this to express my shame towards them. Each person who ever questioned what was going on with me could have done something to help. They all could have confronted Tammie, reported my uncles to the police, and asked me more questions because each of them had an idea that something just was not right. They witnessed, at the very least, the way Tammie would yell at me, call me all kinds of names, and force me to stay in my room, or hit me for very minor problems. Yes, they could have done something.

Instead, they chose to sit by and just let it happen. They became participants, willing participants in the abuse indirectly yet directly. That was the one time they could have chosen to not mind their business. Their silence was not golden. Their silence contributed to my misery and pain. Being called a "snitch" or "tattle teller" for that purpose would have been a great reward. They could have "dropped dime" at any moment for me. Short of beating me themselves, they are just as guilty. Yep, they stood by and did nothing.

I want my book to open the spirit of anyone who sees themselves on these pages to take responsibility for the disconnection they have caused. It is also my desire that whomever the person may be that they will at least try to correct what they have done. Whether it's a military vet who knows he has a child overseas he had never seen, or a social worker who dropped the ball on an adoption case from years ago. Please, stop what you are doing and take steps to correct the mistakes you have made. If there is no way for you to go back and at least try to undo what's been done, then pay it forward.

When I think about the countless news reports of children who are abused by sick-minded adults, I can't help but wonder how anyone could sit back and not do anything to help. What really causes someone to know a child goes to bed exhausted from a ruthless beating and not call to report the crime to the police or other authorities? Why is a child overlooked and allowed to be raped by two different men for nearly 15 years and have her life threatened if she told anyone what she suffered? I pride myself on being a pretty smart woman however this is one thing I just cannot figure out for the life of me!

Everyday, there are people like the ones I described above who knowingly fail to perform their duties. They are family members, friends, neighbors, strangers, municipalities, and even people who work for various government agencies who, for sake of not getting involved, look the other way. They ignore the signs, fail to follow proper procedures, and take short cuts just to lighten their load. They allow a child to be enrolled in school without getting all of the paper-work because "every child deserves an education." They are fearful of challenging what they know to be wrong all because they don't want to get cursed out by the client on their caseload. All of them are equally responsible for every wrongful act that causes damage and harm to innocent children everywhere. In short, these people are what I call Role Players.

Role Players are people who:

- Do not report unexplained cuts, marks, and bruises
- Ignore a child who fearfully cries whenever they are near a particular person
- Witness abuse and shares the account with someone secretly and asks the confidant not to say anything
- Knowingly help an abuser by restraining the child during the abusive act.
- Work for government agencies and school systems but do not follow all procedures designed to accurately identify someone *(Your child can start school today, but you'll need to bring her birth certificate back as soon as possible.)*
- Justifies abuse as "love" <u>(Baby, she didn't mean to hurt you. She just loves you, that's all.)</u>
- Comes to the aid of a child after the abuse promising to help the next time *(If this ever happens again, tell me and I will deal with it.)*
- Claims not to understand why a person abuses a child *(Baby, I don't know why she acts the way she does.)*
- Offers false hope *(It's going to be alright, Honey.)*
- Only disagrees with the severity of the abuse *(I just wish she didn't hit you so hard.)*
- Indirectly blames the child for the abuse they suffer

(Baby, next time, don't do anything that will make her mad.)

- Offers rest as a remedy for your pain *(Baby, just go lay down for a while. You will feel better later.)*
- Discourages the child from telling anyone *(If you tell somebody, your mommy will go to jail and you'll never see her again.)*
- Think it's only abuse if there are signs of "real violence" *(Well, I never saw her slam the child to the ground or nothing like that.)*
- Don't think the person they know could possibly be abusive *(Tammie and I have been friends for over 16 years. She wouldn't hurt a fly.)*
- Sympathizes with you by appearing to be in your corner, on your side, "got your back" but they really want get in your business *(That's a shame that Tammie never told you" or "I don't care what she says: you will always be my cousin.)*
- Decides to just comfort the child the best way they know how *(Here, Baby. Put this money in your pocket and treat yourself to some ice cream later today.)*
- Let you leave the house knowing that you are about to run away from home.

Role Players do what they do because:

- They don't want to get involved for fear of being called a snitch.

- They don't want to break up the family where the abuse is happening.
- They don't want to bring public shame on the family where the abuse is happening.
- They think the problem is too big for them to handle.
- They are afraid the abuser will target their family and seek retaliation.
- They have enough problems of their own and don't have time to deal with someone else's problems.
- They honestly think that they are doing a child a favor.
- They are in denial.
- They decide to just wish it all away.
- They don't think calling the police will make a difference.
- They can't imagine the abused child going into the foster care system.
- They were probably abused as a child and don't have the strength to relive the pain and experience through an abused child.
- The abused child, for the most part, is well fed, dressed nicely, and goes to school everyday.
- They just don't make the time to care.

Each time you turned away blindly all those years ago, you beat me just as hard as Tammie. You even raped me along with my uncles. When I told you I was being touched you acted as if you did not hear or understand. Though time has passed and some wounds have healed, the child in me is scarred for life. Some scars are still extremely painful. Just thinking about them takes me to my knees.

Years have gone by and everyday you say to yourself, "I could have helped. I should have done something to get that child out of the house." Now that you see me as an adult, it causes the pain in both of us to resurface once more. No matter how hard you try to focus on the woman I have become, you can't help but wonder how much smarter, stronger, happier I would be had you intervened. Immediately, you are held responsible for the decision you made to not help, to not get involved.

The memories of that lifetime that you kept in the past smacks you right in the face. And when you finally get a chance to greet me up close, it's not wrapped in kindness or excitement or fond memories. It's awkward and even a bit uncomfortable. Your hug is soft and a bit cold and your kiss is not a kiss at all. You start with the pity in your eyes and then in your voice. It's just like the voice that was there all those years ago. In your ignorance, you let "I had nothing to do with it, you know that right?" slip out of your mouth and then quickly apologize for not knowing what to say at all. It's way too late for apologies because those words have already caused me to flash back to the time of my abuse.

As I look straight into your eyes, right now, today, this very moment, sadness and shame fills my heart. In my mind, there are thoughts of you doing nothing to help me. But now, I realize that you were the one who needed the help. I realize that you were just as scared as I was. Some would say that I am giving you a pass by saying that and you don't have the right to have an excuse. Well, I guess that's just the humane and understanding side of me. Everyone deserves a chance. Either way, it's time for you take ownership and make an amends for what you have done.

I am the book that I read about a little girl being abused, neglected, and stripped of her innocence. I am the song that I sing about a child crying themselves to sleep at night. I am the movie that I go and see about a child walking out of the house that holds nothing but horrible memories and never returning. I am Symbolie Monique Smith. I am the ancestor.

Celie don't have nothing on me. Shucks, I would have taken a "Mista" any day. It's no secret that I have overcome great odds. Easily, I could be dead and gone, strung out on drugs, prostituting for a living, or sleeping on the streets of Baltimore. However, my Creator has helped me to take one day at a time and stay close to him. My healing process began long ago when I learned to forgive you; your healing process will now begin. Unfortunately, there is nothing that can be done to avoid what's to come. Just as I, you too will have to live with the roller coaster of emotions you'll walk away with once we tell each other "Goodbye", Role Player.

Goodbye.